ART & DESIGN

ACADEMY GROUP LTD
42 LEINSTER GARDENS, LONDON W2 3AN
TEL: 0171-402 2141 FAX: 0171-723 9540

EDITOR: Nicola Kearton
ASSISTANT EDITOR: Ramona Khambatta
ART EDITOR: Andrea Bettella
CHIEF DESIGNER: Mario Bettella
DESIGNER: Sonia Brooks-Fisher

SUBSCRIPTION OFFICES:
UK: VCH PUBLISHERS (UK) LTD
8 WELLINGTON COURT, WELLINGTON STREET
CAMBRIDGE CB1 1HZ
TEL: (01223) 321111 FAX: (01223) 313321

USA AND CANADA: VCH PUBLISHERS INC
303 NW 12TH AVENUE DEERFIELD BEACH,
FLORIDA 33442-1788 USA
TEL: (305) 428-5566 / (800) 367-8249
FAX: (305) 428-8201

ALL OTHER COUNTRIES:
VCH VERLAGSGESELLSCHAFT MBH
BOSCHSTRASSE 12, POSTFACH 101161
69451 WEINHEIM
FEDERAL REPUBLIC OF GERMANY
TEL: 06201 606 148 FAX: 06201 606 184

Subscription rates for 1996 (incl p&p): *Annual subscription price*: UK only £65.00, World DM 195 for regular subscribers. *Student rate*: UK only £50.00, World DM 156 incl postage and handling charges. *Individual issues*: £17.95/DM 42.50 (plus £2.30/DM 5 for p&p, per issue ordered).
For the USA and Canada: *Art & Design* is published six times per year (Jan/Feb; Mar/Apr; May/Jun; Jul/Aug; Sept/Oct; and Nov/Dec) by Academy Group Ltd, 42 Leinster Gardens, London W2 3AN, England and distributed by VCH Publishers, Inc., 303 N.W. 12th Avenue, Deerfield Beach, FL 33442-1788; Telefax (305) 428 8201; Telephone (305) 428-5566 or (800) 367 8249. Annual subscription price; US $135.00 including postage and handling charges; special student rates available at $105.00, single issue $28.95. Second-class postage paid at Deerfield Beach, Fl 33441. **POSTMASTER**: Send address changes to Art & Design, c/o VCH Publishers, Inc., 303 N.W. 12th Avenue, Deerfild Beach FL 33442-1788.
Printed in Italy. All prices are subject to change without notice. [ISSN: 0267-3991]
The full text of *Art & Design* is also available in the electronic versions of the Art Index.

CONTENTS

Ruth Stirling, *Miracle*, 1995.
Photo: Renzo Mazzolini

Fine Rats International,
Francis Gomila, *Under Spaghetti Junction*, 'Bathing in Recession', 1993, Birmingham

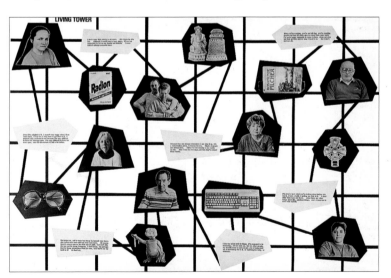

Stephen Willats, *Living Tower*, 1993, Hammersmith, London

Trying to get on with my own way of life.

How can I maintain my real values within such regular surroundings.

Searching for domestic harmony within contained conditions.

How can we enjoy our privacy while extending life at home.

Striving all our working life against economic forces.

How can we afford the environment we would like for our family.

Attempting to establish our own cultural life.

How can I find a way of expressing myself with my neighbours.

Learning to Live within a Confined Space, *February – April 1978, photographic prints, gouache, ink, Letraset on card, four panels, each 100 x 132cm*

STEPHEN WILLATS

An interview with Nicola Kearton

Born in London, Stephen Willats became active in the conceptual art scene in London in the 1960s, working with residents of council estates and housing developments throughout Europe to produce highly collaborative pieces in which he takes the role of instigator rather than creator/author. Academy Editions is publishing Stephen Willats: Between Buildings and People *in April 1996 which explores, through the medium of the artist's own work, the experiences of people living in these often highly stigmatised environments.*

Nicola Kearton: For over 30 years you have been creating interactive works within the community which involve the public directly. What were your dissatisfactions in the early 60s with the gallery and museum system?

Stephen Willats: It is really best seen against a background of trying to break through the taboos and constrictions of the culture of the 50s, a world that was heavily restricted in what people thought was possible. I was one of many who saw that it was fruitful to make interactions with other people in other areas, other realms of creative thought and behaviour. It was also apparent that the kind of world we expected to move into was going to be more interactive, non-hierarchical, self-organising. There was a general feeling of progress towards something which was going to benefit everybody, although nobody knew quite what this thing was that we were progressing towards. I was part of that original generation of so-called 'angry young men' who felt that they could strip away all the restrictions of the post-war world. I felt right from the outset that art fundamentally is a social phenomenon that takes place in society. The audience is therefore a fundamental part of the work, and the work of art itself is a pragmatic communication between artist and audience. There is therefore no separation both theoretically and actually between the artist and the nature of social context in which art is going to operate. This was a feeling that was heretical at the time and largely remains so today.

NK: You have also mentioned that the language of art and art history was inadequate to express work which was moving beyond the confines of the art world.

SW: Well, I think perhaps that gradually dawned on people who initially tried to establish new kinds of practices using the existing, shall we say, the recent history of art as a parameter to what they were doing. People started to see that there were other areas of society where people were thinking about communication and to appropriate what could be appropriated back into the realm of

art. Information theory, cybernetics, cognitive psychology and these territories of research, were embryonic at that point. The 'Mechanisation of Thought Process' symposium in the late 50s at the National Physical Laboratory was a mind-blowing breakthrough for everyone. This was the advent of early computing technology, and philosophy that forwarded the idea that we might look at reality as an actual construction of the brain. There was a feeling that all this was going towards creating a physical and social reality which reflected different models of control than those that had existed previously. These models of control were essentially self-organising models – dynamic, interactive, evolving, changing, responsive – a marked contrast to a world which had seemed pre-set and fossilised.

NK: How did the idea of exploring modernist architecture and the way people related to living and working within this type of environment come about?

SW: Well, I think the thing again is, of course, that modernist architecture was identified with a modern way of life which was seen then to offer non-hierarchical and socially interactive posibilities. Before modern building became heavily stigmatised, it was associated with more communal social models of existence. In the late 50s and early 60s, they just seemed icons of the future and many of us felt that this kind of physical reality would involve quite different social structures. This, of course, did not turn out to be the case, but that was the feeling.

NK: How did you find people related to the idea of working with you as an artist in their own environment? Did you find there was a problem with intention or language?

SW: Well, I have evolved a methodology of working with people over a very long period of time. It originally came out of this feeling that art should engage with the infrastructure of society, that it should develop a function that is positive and forward-looking and which can represent different ideological models of reality back to society. In other words it was an intervening role.

NK: Haven't you written on the role of the artist as instigator rather than creator of a work of art?

SW: In the early 70s I wrote a paper which was published by Gallery House Press called 'The Artist as an Instigator of Changes in Social Cognition And Behaviour', and this really sums up my approach and decision in the mid 60s to see that art should go beyond the art gallery and the museum. What was important was the meaning of the work and its message, so the form itself was pragmatically dictated by the content. When I first started working with people, one of the works I made was on a housing estate in Ipswich in 1965 which was full of London over-spill. Working with a group of students, we had the idea to make a work from scratch, to presume nothing about a work of art, only that we desired to make one. How would we approach this? Who was going to be the audience for this work? What was the work going to say? So, what we did here was to define a group of people who would be the audience of the work and who we thought the work could have some meaning for, and involve them in a positive way. The next thing was how to evolve a language which would be meaningful to this audience. When I was working within the art institution, one could tend to assume that the audience was versed in the languages of art and knew what was going on. When you vary those constraints to operate beyond the confines of the art museum, it can be quite interesting, quite disastrous, or quite re-appraising.

NK: Were you influenced by any contemporary linguistic theory?

SW: In this particular work at Ipswich and then later in the 60s and early 70s, I was very much influenced by the work of Basil Bernstein who developed the idea of Restricted Codes, and I saw that perhaps what I should embody in the language of the art work were the codes which were already meaningful to the group of people who were the audience. At Ipswich the students and I therefore conducted a research project with a questionnaire in which we asked people various questions about the colour of their front door, the shape of things on their mantlepiece, and we attempted to build up from this a language for the work. At the same time, we were also trying to find what was missing in people's experience of this environment that they found themselves in. What we found was that, very simply, people did not know where anything was and so we decided that the work should redirect people to things that were important to them. We then made a series of sign posts which we set up around the estate – for instance, there was an area which was dangerous for children to play in because of quicksand, so we made danger signs using Bernstein's ideas about signals. We also made signs out of shopping produce to point the way to the supermarket. What was interesting was that these signs stayed in position for quite a long while.

NK: They were actually useful.

SW: Yes, and what was important to me personally, and subsequently shaped a lot of my approach, was that when meaning was found by the audience in the work of art to be relevant to themselves, then their acceptance and engagement with it was entirely different from when they could not see what was going on. This also separated my approach from people who have tried to externalise art beyond the museum but have merely taken practices which have evolved within the museum and placed them outside.

NK: This, of course, brings to mind the controversy over Richard Serra's *Tilted Arc* which was removed due to pressure from the local office workers.

SW: Well, that is a very good example and no wonder people felt closed in, their psychology was infringed on a way they could not accept. I have realised that to work with people, you enter into a kind of interactive engagement. For example, when I was working with pieces like *The West London Social Resource Project*, I tried all kinds of approaches: I took out advertisements in newspapers, put leaflets through people's doors, or tried phoning people. None of these things work as well as when you simply go along and talk to somebody. In the end the only way I could involve people was to knock on their doors. I would explain the project and then there was a one in two chance of someone showing some kind of interest and from there, one in two actually became involved in the project and went through with the work. So what I am trying to say here is that although my engagements in essence are very simple ones, and adhere to the norms and conventions of interpersonal behaviour, you need a long time to get their real involvement, you cannot force people, you cannot rush them.

NK: Hence you have had to show a strong commitment to a place and your projects have taken years to make in some cases.

SW: Yes, a work might take some nine months to prepare even though the actual presentation of it might be, say, over 14 days. This is why time is used as a constructive element that allows many of my works to start with models of descriptive reality before moving towards models which involve people in changing that reality. So there is a learning curve where you start with what is closest to a person before moving away towards something more ideologically removed from how they are at that moment.

NK: Do you see your art as a sort of healing process? A lot of artists, especially those involved in public art works, talk about their art as having a healing aspect?

SW: No, these works are, if anything, going in the opposite direction and are intended to empower people to realise that they have the possibility of their own creative self-organisation within them to change their circumstances. It is more a re-awakening of the feeling of the power of community and people.

NK: *Vertical Living* had the effect of creating a community out of an enormous vertical structure where people felt very isolated on separate floors.

SW: Well, it had a positive effect but it was not a remedial effect, which would be like trying to put the cap on the existing situation. *Vertical Living* dynamically shook up the whole social relationship within the structure of the tower block in a way the authorities were not particularly happy with. People started to set up their own organisations and to use each other's flats as offices for these organisations. But it is really the effect on people individually that was important. The work, and other works as well, have had the intended effect of introducing people to the realisation that their perception is utterly relative. Thus I do not say 'no' to anyone – if anyone wants to work with me, they can do so.

NK: So you act completely randomly in that respect.

SW: Yes, if someone wants to work with me, then through discussion and my engagement with that person, I find something that that person really wants to say and my role is to bring that out and allow them to develop it. But there is a topology to the relationship. People come to make a work of art and thus I am not involved in the whole area of their lives necessarily.

NK: So the idea of it being a work of art is important to give parameters to what you are doing, otherwise it could be confusing – you are not a social worker or a doctor.

SW: Well, it is very important that people feel that you are an artist, someone in their world that perhaps is not exactly neutral but whom they have not come across before and who does not have an axe to grind. Some years ago I conducted a piece of research with Kevin Lole where we went around various housing estates with a questionnaire which questioned people's perceptions of art and artists. These were people that did not visit art galleries and museums very much. We found that even in the most remote location, people still have a model of art and artists that is important to them, even if it is a model of art that is quite clearly different from how most artists see themselves. It is important to them to have some notion of someone out there, who is outside the system.

NK: Some notion that artists are not 'functionaries' of the system?

SW: Maybe this is one of the reasons that when I am working with people I find they do not say 'Ah, this is a crazy project' or something like that – they want to get involved in it. It is quite interesting that although I have always had this very negative response from officialdom, what in the end amazes them is that these works operate. For instance on this piece *Private Journeys*, I made recently, on the Heston Farm Estate in Hayes, West London, I was working in an incredibly negative climate in a place that was heavily stigmatised and seen very much as being the end of the line. When I came to present the work after my being on the estate for a year-and-a-half, I took over the community room at the centre of the estate. I set up my installation and from the start I had an extremely volatile situation. But people did start to engage with the work, and when after five days it came to an end, more or less the whole estate had in some way or the other been involved in the piece to a point where they did not want it to stop. The local authorities were quite amazed really, they did not think anything like this could have happened, and the result was that they felt confident about doing something else there.

NK: You have talked a lot in your work about the idea of a journey and a transformation between different realities, I am thinking particularly of *Pat Purdy and the Glue Sniffers' Camp*.

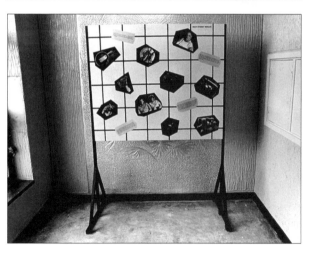

FROM ABOVE: Public Register Board, remodelling book response, West London Resource Project, Osterley Library, 1972-73; Contained Living, Friars Wharf Estate, Oxford, 1976; Multi-storey Mosaic, Feltham, West London, 1989

V

SW: I see transformation as a very fundamental creative act from one thing into another; and the journey itself can be seen as a medium for an act of transformation which enables one psychology to go into another psychology. When I was making work in the early 80s – the *Doppelganger* series for instance – what I noticed was the idea that within the self there were different states that exist in a kind of parallel co-existence and that one oscillates between different parts of one's own psychology. With *Pat Purdy and the Glue Sniffers' Camp*, it was the walks into the wasteland which were the medium for the transformation. Here, the fence separating the Avondale estate from the relative freedom of the surrounding wasteland was the point where you went from one to the other, the hole in the fence, like a re-birth. You construct reality and project it onto what is there and so I think the idea of the journey is that it really is symbolic. It is rather like saying 'art in the 60s was manifesto led'. If you are going to vary norms and conventions, it is difficult to do without some logical construction, you need some logical rationale, even though this may disappear immediately after the event. So, in a way, the journey is the logical construction that enables you to move from one state to the other state. I was also interested in the way that people transported objects as a sort of vehicle for this transformation. In the case of *Pat Purdy* there was the highly symbolic object – the can of glue. Here it was associated in one part of the world positively with sticking things together, and in another, the wasteland, in creating a community. For when people went into the wasteland to construct camps, it was a social activity, they did not do it on their own.

I am fascinated by this idea of the journey, and I see it in many different forms: whether it is the idea of Pat Purdy going into the wasteland, or somebody looking out of a window in a tower block, they are making a kind of cognitive or mental journey from inside their living space into the reality around them.

NK: We have talked about how you have moved away from the institutions of art, but on the other hand, rather than just moving out of the gallery or museum, you seem to have taken real life and actually gone back into the museum or gallery with it. Was this a conscious decision on your part?

SW: I have always operated as, and considered myself to be an artist, and in the early 70s I decided to work with the institutions of art whilst attempting to change their topology. I saw that the art museum itself could become an interactive entity within the world around it, and that within the art museum could be represented the polemics, issues and reality of the world outside. For instance, one particular work at the Museum of Modern Art in Oxford, *Contained Living*, was made between the Friars Wharf Housing Estate and the museum. The work itself was an interactive work in two parts, so one part was situated on the estate, and the other part in the museum, so people coming to the museum went to the housing estate and people from the housing estate went to the museum to complete their engagement with the work. People living on the estate had never been to the Museum of Modern Art,

even though it was only a quarter-of-a-mile up the road.

It was a work that people living on the estate had constructed with me and it took about nine months to develop. Again the authorities said 'Ah, you know, you're wasting your time Mr Willats', and I must say I was very nervous. I remember when we put our first display board up at the centre of Friars Wharf Estate – just two sticks in the ground with a photographic board in between which a gust of wind could have blown away, but it never got vandalised. In fact, every day another element was added to it and people from the estate began to visit the museum and vice versa. It was quite an amazing transformation of the space in the museum. So I am interested in working with art institutions, not to see them as containers of authoritative icons, but to see them as pragmatic tools that we can use to engage an audience.

NK: What do you think about recent experiments in public art?
SW: Well, I think that what is important at the moment, and it makes this particular discussion more pertinent than at other points in time, is that there is now a general cultural climate which is moving towards the idea of a more interactively based society.

NK: Would you say that people are now engaging with these ideas from the 60s but taking them further?
SW: They are taking them further in a way but that they are not so ideologically led, the ideology seems to be missing. There does seem to be another atmosphere, another attitude which is emerging out of the possibilities of communication. So, I think what is happening at the moment is that there is a very exciting development in culture and especially in art where people are beginning to set up new models of practice which are engaged directly with the world around. The infrastructure and the containment of art within authoritatively legitimised institutions is being broken down. However, this is not being authoritatively led from above, it is just happening through the infrastructure itself becoming interactive.

NK: Would you like to talk about the main premise of the book we are preparing, *Stephen Willats: Between Buildings and People*?
SW: I would like to see it as a handbook really, about my one person experience of trying to engage with this physical and social world that we are in. But it is also seen as a tool to provide a realm of information about a territory of references and procedures that certainly in terms of art and anybody wanting to work with people and buildings, largely does not exist. What might be interesting from the point of view of an architect is to take another look at it from the point of view of how someone else, such as myself, has approached this. An important feature of the book is also that we have testimonies from people who live in those architects' visions of the new reality of modernist building. So there are two realities relative to each other, we have the reality of the architect whose plan, vision, is realised in an actual building. But in this book, we have the testimony of people's experience of those buildings, so I think this is what is very interesting.

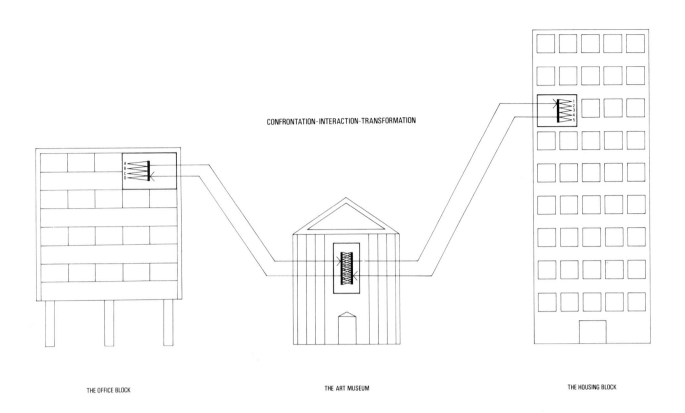

CONFRONTATION-INTERACTION-TRANSFORMATION

THE OFFICE BLOCK   THE ART MUSEUM   THE HOUSING BLOCK

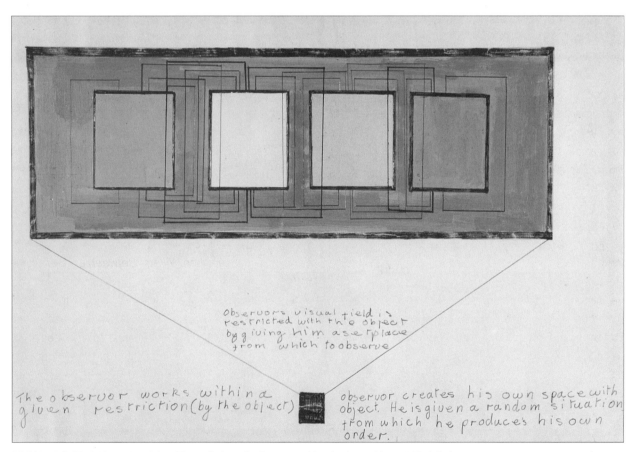

FROM ABOVE: A Work Involving Three Culturally Separated Institutions, *May 1987, Ink, Letraset text on paper, 57 x 73cm. This drawing proposes the museum as an interactive agency between different external, social and physical environments. The museum provides the Meta Language and the means of achieving perceptibly transformation;* Drawing to a Colour Variable, No 1, *1962*

Stephen Willats: Between Buildings and People, *Academy Editions, Paperback 1 85490 436 1, £17.95, 252 x 190mm, 144 pages, Over 100 black & white illustrations, Date of Publication: April 1996*

HIDE AND SEEK
Laurent Tixador

At the end of 1994 the headmaster of the Joliot Curie infant school in Waziers, France, invited me to to suggest a piece of work the school could buy which would serve as a basis for art lessons and the study of colour and form. Instead of providing an existing work from the studio, I suggested an *in situ* piece that could be built in the playground. In order to overcome a limited budget, we established an unusual direct partnership with the town's works department who provided the materials and carried out the work.

The plane trees in the playground provided the starting point for a work in which I continued my investigation of confrontation of colour (here, specifically sugary tones like childrens' sweets) and frontiers – the gaps in the pieces were based on the silhouette line of the tree next to it. The work is visible through the school gates from the outside and provides a study of colour and image, framed by the trees, the model and its painting.

For the schoolchildren the piece serves a very different purpose. Classic French playgrounds are designed specifically to ensure the children can always be seen. Naturally this facilitates the task of the teacher on duty. However, it is very difficult for the children to get away from each other and from the teacher, not only physically, but mentally. I still remember the satisfaction of being able to escape, for even a few seconds, during play time.

The work is entitled *La Douane des pensées* (Borderline of Thought). It provides the opportunity for children to play hide and seek, and at the same time, to see through the gap, to cross another frontier, to step for a moment into their own world, alone for just a few seconds and yet quite safe and able to relate to the work for their own imaginative purposes.

CULTURE IN ACTION, Sculpture Chicago, with essays by Mary Jane Jacob, Michael Brenson, Eva M Olson, Bay Press, Seattle, 1995, 144pp, PB £N/A

The prime mover behind the two-year 'Culture in Action' project, Mary Jane Jacob has clearly questioned the value of traditional approaches to public art and spoken forcefully in favour of change as one well-versed in the language of art criticism and discourse.

The success of these highly varied art projects underlines the value of questioning established public art practices and this is well-documented by accounts of the processes involved in their making. For Mary Jane Jacob, 'process' is all-important as is the need to question our perceptions and pre-conceptions at all times. The organisation behind 'Culture in Action', 'Sculpture Chicago', is an unconventional institution truly belonging in the public realm and, according to its Director Eva Olson, is 'committed to defining a new form of public art (with) equal emphasis on artist and audience', and aims for a form of art that 'fosters dialogue through communal action'. As the interview with Mary Jane Jacob in this issue reveals, much of the debate revolves around the nature of the art object: where it begins and ends, where it belongs and what meaning it has for its audience and/or curator(s). This is fully explored in the book's accounts of community/artist partnerships which resulted in artworks as diverse as a 'storefront hydrophonic garden' and 'a new line of candy'. As a document of challenging contemporary public art methodology, this book provides a provocative starting point in a debate recently fuelled by controversy which seems set to run and run. PH

BILAN DES RENCONTRES, edited by Yves Nacher, Institut français d'architecture, PB FF75

This edition concludes the 'Art & Ville' programme, a cycle of professional seminars which took place in different regions of France in 1993 and 1994, organised by the Institut français d'architecture at the request of the Ministère de l'équipement, the Ministère de la culture and other bodies connected with urban development and architecture. The publication is presented as a series of case studies demonstrating the variety of the public art commissions and other urban projects carried out by over 500 participants. These are accompanied by texts from architects, town-planners, artists, art critics and philosophers on the question of the role and actions of public authorities in the fabrication of the city and the emergence of a new urban aesthetic.

This volume can be ordered from Institut français d'architecture, 6 rue de Tournon, 75006 Paris. Tel: 1-46 33 90 36   Fax: 1-46 33 02 11   AC

PICTURE THEORY, Essays on Verbal and Visual Representation by WJT Mitchell, University of Chicago Press, Chicago and London, 1994, 462pp, HB (only to order) £27.95 PB £13.50

A fascinating and insightful study of the much-debated, yet inextricable, link between words and pictures, WJT Mitchell examines this partnership in the context of the late twentieth century. The analysis is examined at several levels, including philosophy (Ludwig Wittgenstein), poetry and art (William Blake), photography (Walter Evans and James Agee) and one of the most accessible art forms today – film. The final chapter of the book, 'Pictures and the Public Sphere', concentrates on two films – Oliver Stone's *JFK* and Spike Lee's *Do the Right Thing* – and discusses how through a popular and very much public media, words and pictures can influence debate and new theories in society, shaping entirely new public views.

Picture Theory is written with zest and covers such a wide spectrum of ideas and examples that it serves to appeal to a public across the board, lowering the barrier which many believe is erected by a vast number of art theory books. RK

QUEUES RENDEZVOUS RIOTS by George Baird and Mark Lewis, Walter Phillips Gallery, The Banff Centre for the Arts, 1994, 176pp, 43 b/w ills, 6 colour ills, HB, $35.00

This book, edited by the curators, is based on an exhibition in 1992 at the Walter Phillips Gallery in Banff, Canada and deals with the question of 'the public' in art and architecture. Essays from the participants in the exhibition include Rodolfo Machado and Jorge Silvetti, Vera Frenkel, Elizabeth Diller and Richard Scofidio and others. The present pre-occupation with all things public – in cultural, commercial and political industries – is particularly clear in art and architecture. Debates continue to unfold in competitions for architectural projects over what form of expression may be considered appropriate. The Machado and Silvetti project entitled *Banffire* consisted of a stone fire pit set in front of Donald Cameron Hall, marked by a metal sculpture representing the skull of a colossal elk. Using fire, not water, as the centre of attention for public art and a hearth-like device to attract a gathering in lieu of the traditional fountain was remarkable. The fire was accepted by the jury, the elk, however was not because it was considered 'inappropriate' for the institution. One of the most inspired essays entitled 'Questioning the Public: Addressing the Response', was not from one of the artists or architects but from a commentator, Johanne Lamoureux. She addressed the absurdity of an exhibition raising the issue of 'the public' in a venue such as the gallery at the Banff Centre for the Arts, and nowhere else. The Banff Centre for the Arts is a closed circuit utopian art community. The appropriateness of the exhibition: site, title, install-ations was hotly debated by critics and in-house artists. This debating in the book sometimes comes across as negative but at other times as therapeutic criticism. CF

THE BENEFITS OF PUBLIC ART: The Polemics of Permanent Art in Public Places, by Sara Selwood, Policy Studies Institute, London, 1995, 367pp, b&w ills, £17.95

This ground-breaking study analyses the impact of public art in Britain during the past 15 years, looking at available statistics, funding of projects, comparisons between projects – for example those commissioned in the private and public sectors – and means for judging quality and general success of contemporary public art. It attempts to look behind the 'myth' of public art, asking whether it is an environmental improver, as often claimed, what contributions artists have to offer beyond those of other professionals, who is accountable for public art and by whose standards should it be judged. On the basis of seven case studies which highlight key problems with public commissions, Selwood's recom-mendations for those involved in

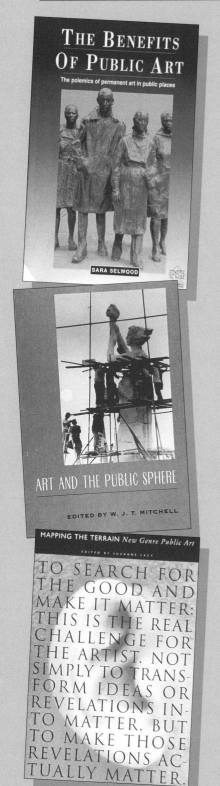

ART ET MEGALOPOLE – R.N. 86 l'Institut pour l'Art et la Ville (in French), Feb 1996, FF N/A

Since 1989 the Institut pour l'Art et la Ville, Givors has been working on possible relationships between art, architecture and the city. The Route Nationale 86, a main road from Paris to the South of France, crosses the town of Givors. In 1993, the restructuring of this main road provided the opportunity to set up a programme of both temporary and permanent art projects; six artists were invited to contribute their ideas. The book entitled *Art et Mégalopole, R.N. 86* (to be published in February 1996) which includes art projects by Mierle Laderman Ukeles, Catherine Beaugrand, Simon Patterson, Rémy Zaugg, Michel Desvigne and Antonio Muntadas serves as a basis for theoretical texts on the relationship between art and urban development today. Authors include James Lingwood, of the Artangel Trust, Tom Finkelpearl, responsible for the one per cent programme in New York City, Jacky Vieux, director of the Institut pour l'Art et la Ville, and Alain Charre, scientific advisor of the Institut.

Other publications by the Institute include *Art et espaces publics*, 1992, 137FF and *Cahiers* (published three times a year). For further information, contact Jacky Vieux, Director, Institut pour l'Art et la Ville, La Maison du Rhône, 1 place de la Liberté, 69700 Givors, France. Tel: 78 73 70 37 Fax: 78 07 14 63   AC

ART AND THE PUBLIC SPHERE edited by WJT Mitchell, The University of Chicago Press, Chicago and London, 1992, 280pp, HB (only to order) £37.25 PB £15.95

This seminal volume of 13 essays by leading critics, authors and artists, addresses recent controversies in public art, focusing on historical, symbolic, political, legal and cultural concerns. The essays draw upon examples of public art which excite such reactions and then explore the reasons for this conflict of interest. WJT Mitchell examines the violence of public art, citing such examples as the destruction of the Mao Tse-tung's statue at Beijing University, which ignited similarly aggressive behaviour throughout China, culminating in Tiananmen Square where Mao's statue was disfigured and a 30-foot-high styrofoam and

plaster 'Goddess of Liberty' was erected directly opposite – an image of peace and equality, but one which reflects a multitude of undertones alluding to violence. Mitchell argues that public outrage against public art on such an extreme level is not a contemporary phenomenon, but one which dates back to antiquity. James E Young takes this aspect of public art one step further by examining it in the form of counter-monuments, best exemplified by Holocaust memorial work in Germany. Young exposes the 'tortured, self-reflective, even paralysing preoccupation' – the burden of guilt – the vast majority of the German people feel they have to pay for. He draws our attention to countless examples, including Sol Lewitt's *Skulpture Projekte 87* in Münster, Jochen Gerz and Esther Shalev-Gerz's *Harburg Monument against Fascism* in Hamburg, 1989, and Horst Hoheisel's negative-form monument to the Ascrott-Brunnen in Kassel, 1984. Charles L Griswold follows Young's essay with an essay on what on first impression strikes one as a very different kind of memorial to the dead – The Vietnam Veteran's Memorial in Washington DC. The memorial does not commemorate the dead in a blaze of glory and heroism; its clean lines, the gentle slope into the land, the serenity and simplicity of its form evokes the deepest of emotions which encourage one to reflect upon the futility and loss of aggression. This is a memorial that caused tremendous controversy and Griswold deals with the issue successfully and objectively, leaving the images of the monument to appeal to the emotions. Agnes Denes's essay tackles the issue of public art from a considerably different angle, directing our attention away from war and human-human violence. Her essay targets the artist's role in an age of breathtakingly fast-moving technology where 'hard-won knowledge accumulates undigested, blocking meaningful communication'. Denes believes that the artist's responsibility is to question the status quo and 'the endless contradictions we accept and approve of', and illustrates this through her various works, including the symbolic *Wheatfield – A Confrontation*, 1982, a two-acre wheatfield which she planted in lower Manhattan to call attention to, whilst at the same time balancing, the all-

encompassing evidence of technology and science. One of the last essays is by Richard Serra, the artist, which discusses art and censorship in the light of the political and legislative history of the United States – an issue he has considerable knowledge about, following the US government's destruction of Serra's *Tilted Arc* in 1989. Other contributors include: John Hallmark Neff, Michael North, Barbara Hoffman, Virginia Maksymowicz, Vito Acconci, Ben Nicholson and David Antin.   RK

MAPPING THE TERRAIN: New Genre Public Art, edited by Suzanne Lacy, Art/Cultural Studies, Bay Press, Seattle, 1995, 296pp, £14.99

This volume presents an alternative history to the now accepted lineage of public art progressing from objects in museums, to objects in public places, to site-specific installations. In her introduction, Suzanne Lacy argues that a different interpretation of the history of the last 30 years results in the identifying of a whole body of work that has hitherto been unconnected with the public art debate dominated as it was by sculpture. The key aspect of what she and the contributors describe as 'New Genre' public art is based on engagement with issues that have a direct impact on people's lives, such as pollution, race relations, homelessness, AIDs. Including contributions by Mary Jane Jacob, Patricia Phillips, Suzi Gablik, Guillermo Gömez-Peña, Lucy Lippard and Allen Kaprow, this is a formidable attempt to flesh out a history of art made outside traditional venues using languages of social activism and politics. Recent projects are seen as part of a continuing history of work produced since the 60s by artists such as Joseph Beuys, Vito Acconci, Judy Chicago. Also included is a detailed compendium of nearly 90 artists who represent a broad range of practices, methodologies and ideology which turns a fascinating discursive study into a valuable tool for further research. As Lacy suggests 'the tremendous recent interest in engaged, caring public art demands a context in art history and present criticism. It demands as well the guidance of predecessors who can pass on strategies that allow the wheel to move forward, not suffer endless reinvention.'   NK

funding and promoting public art include greater openness and accountability, increased consultation with the public, more information and interpretation, greater legal clarity and evaluation along with professional development where needed.   NK

LE TRAMWAY DE STRASBOURG

A showcase example of contemporary artists and public art being used to practical and dynamic effect, the recent redevelopment of Le Tramway de Strasbourg provided the ideal opportunity to install public works of art at symbolic or pertinent intervals. Using a variety of artists and media, the tramway system was to be integrated as fully as possible into the social and cultural fabric of the town itself, in a way that would stimulate the passengers and the passers-by alike. The work of the chosen artists achieves this aesthetic synergy with aplomb. Overhead, Jonathan Borofsky brings the power of sculpture, his *Femme marchant vers le ciel* stepping boldly forth above the tram-tracks and rooftops. Mario Merz brings drama to the ground, with illuminated flagstones on the track creating an airport runway effect. In the central station, Barbara Kruger delivers her usual visually and morally dynamic messages on steps and advertising spaces, while out on the pavements, Jean-Michel Wilmotte's infrastructural elements, such as the 'service and information columns', also provide space for the writing of members of Oulipo (a creative movement founded in the 1960s). The aesthetic experience is taken down to the most utilitarian level: even the tickets, collectable items designed by Collin-Thiébaut, bear provocative cultural images with their depictions of scenes of the town, past and present. Curiosity is aroused at every turn, and we are shown that the anonymous and mechanistic process of public transport can and should be a stimulating and very personal experience.

A detailed and well illustrated appraisal of this project is given in *Le Tramway de Strasbourg* by Catherine Grout, Carnets de la Commande Publique, Editions du Regard, Paris, 1995.
(Lucy Ryan)

OPPOSITE: Mario Merz, installation, Rue de la Division Leclerc; FROM ABOVE, L to R: Barbara Kruger installation artwork at the tram terminal building. Photo: C Laurent Lecat; Place de l'Homme de Fer; Gérard Collin-Thiébaut, Tram tickets. Photo: C Laurent Lecat; Jonathan Borofsky, Femme marchant vers le ciel (Woman Walking to the Sky). Photo: C Laurent Lecat; Barbara Kruger artwork at the tram terminal building. Photo (below right): C Laurent Lecat

Book reviews were compiled by:
Sonia Brooks-Fisher
Amanda Crabtree
Cristina Fontoura
Peter Hinton
Nicola Kearton
Ramona Khambatta
Annamarie Uhr Delia

ART ON FILE INTERNATIONAL, 1995 catalogue, 67pp, PB, £ N/A

An annual production, this catalogue lists a vast variety of slides and digital images covering public art, architecture, landscape architecture and urban design in Europe and the United States. Any of these images can be hired throughout the world and a straightforward, user-friendly order form is included at the back of the volume. Each work of art is under its appropriate, clearly labelled category heading, stating artist, whereabouts, information about the piece and a code number to enable easy referencing and ordering. Each category listing is preceded with a black and white photograph of a relevant work and a general introduction, familiarisng the reader with the concept in hand. *Art on File* covers both established works of art as well as new ones which have only recently been completed. This is an invaluable source book, which will not only be of vital help to those who need to borrow images, but also to those interested in finding out what is available and where it exists.

Available from the Public Art Development Trust, 3rd Floor, Kirkman House, 12-14 Whitfiled Street, London W1P 5RD. Tel: 0171-580 9977 Fax: 0171-580 8540   RK

THE HIRSCH FARM PROJECT

A ten-year experimental forum for the discussion of public art, the environment and community, the Hirsch Farm project is an attempt to see what happens if a group of artists is brought together to develop ideas rather than produce objects. It has now broadened its objectives to include a range of professionals from the arts, sciences and humanities who meet once a year for a week in rural Wisconsin in order to discuss in depth a particular topic of importance to the visual arts. Following each meeting the participants prepare essays, project proposals or artists' pages which are included in a book produced by the Hirsch Farm Project and distributed internationally to professionals in a wide variety of disciplines. The result

is that this artist-driven think tank, directed by Mitchell Kane, is becoming increasingly influential in the field of public art and contemporary art in general. Recent volumes include *Pressure on the Public*, 1992, *NonSpectacle and the Limitations of Popular Opinion*, 1993 and *Optimism* 1994.

For further information contact Laurie Winter, Hirsch Foundation, 450 Skokie Blvd, Suite 703, Northbrook II, 60062. Tel: 708 480 2000 Fax: 708 480 2005.   NK

ART WITH PEOPLE, Artists Handbooks, Malcolm Dickson, AN Publications, Sunderland, 1995, pp136, PB £N/A

Art with People is funded by The Arts Council of England, tracing the history of community art, from its conception in the 60s to modern day issues. It takes public art as a greater whole and explains how this particular field of art involves the whole community, covering art in education, the pioneers, art in prison, residencies and community arts; whilst focusing more closely on art which has allowed the community, including women, the disabled, gays, blacks and Aids sufferers to be acknowledged. *Art with People* challenges future relationships between artists and the public, asking the eternally debated question, 'who is art for?'   SBF

SYDNEY SPACES, 29 Concepts for the City's Streets, Squares and Parks, Sydney City Council, 1995, illustrated in colour, 72pp, PB £N/A

This beautifully produced publication accompanies the Sydney City Council's 'Living City' initiative. The Lord Mayor of Sydney, Councillor Frank Sartor reflects that, 'for too long Sydney has relied on the physical beauty of its setting' and in line with the Council's commitment to enhancing the public realm, over 30 architects, landscape architects and artists were invited to develop proposals for various spaces throughout Sydney's centre. 'Living City's' project director, Helen

Lockhead, introduces the projects which have been divided into two main categories. The first reinforce the nature of the place by subtle re-adjustment, while the second deals with areas which demand more radical intervention. From traffic calming and pedestrian zones to connecting squares or dramatic sculptural events, the projects include concepts by Tony Caro, William Morrison, Gillian Smart and Peter Tonkin. Each concept is presented with a written description briefly outlining the significance of the site and the intended design. This is well supported with the Architects/Planners drawings (mostly in colour), alongside technical details and plans. The location of each project is mapped onto a aerial photograph of the central Sydney, which shows the linkage of sites to great effect.

As fear and debate about urban conformity and the homogenisation of modern cities takes the world forum, *Sydney Spaces* attempts to redefine the requirements of the city for both inhabitants and visitors, as Sydney approaches the new millennium and the international spectacle of the 2000 Olympics. James Colman's introductory essay, 'A City Tells us Things', briefly explores the growth from penal colony to thriving commercial and tourist centre and the planning, or in some respects the lack of it, that has determined the physical presence of Sydney's urban fabric. Possessing some of the most recognisable landmarks cradled by the stunning aspect of Sydney Harbour, Colman argues that it is the interactivity or linkage between sites as well as the enhancement of open spaces and concern for the quality of public places that will generate an exciting city in which to live. The city should encourage involvement and be experienced rather than viewed. Although the projects in this book are based on places in Sydney the concepts are applicable in any city that is looking to re-involve its inhabitants in the experience of its urban fabric and to generate a living growing city for the future.   AUD

What is...?

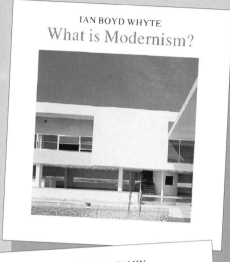

New Edition
WHAT IS POST-MODERNISM?
Fourth Edition
Charles Jencks

What is Post-Modernism? A question that has been asked with increasing frequency over the last 25 years, now achieves a partial answer as it continues to evolve. In the fourth edition of his book Charles Jencks, the main definer of Post-Modern architecture, considers the concept as it relates to the arts and literature and offers a spirited defence of the movement against the growing Modernist reaction. This completely revised text presents the reader with numerous new examples of art and architecture appropriate to the theme and outlines the history which preceded Post-Modernism, facilitating a much clearer understanding of the overall concept.

PB 1 85490 428 0
240 x 225mm, 68 pages
70 illustrations, mostly in colour
June 1996

WHAT IS ABSTRACTION ?
Andrew Benjamin

Continuing our *What is . . . ?* series this text addresses the question of abstraction, one of the most significant and influential schools of criticism, by looking at three interconnected projects. The first argues that developments within abstraction have rendered the traditional theoretical and philosophical understandings of abstraction inadequate. The second develops the theoretical and philosophical issues in relation to contemporary abstract work and the third shows in what way these theoretical innovations allow for the reinterpretation of the tradition of abstraction.

PB 1 85490 434 5
240 x 225mm, 68 pages
Illustrated throughout
April 1996

WHAT IS MODERNISM?
Ian Boyd Whyte

Modernism has dominated architectural theory and practice for most of this century. The International Style, which emerged at the beginning of this century partly as a reaction against Victorian high style, produced many sleek, elegant buildings. The architectural reaction to this incredible social movement which swept through all aspects of society was to provide good, low-cost public housing. This, the fourth in the *What is . . . ?* series explains Modernism in an illuminating and accessible way. Many examples are used to illustrate this movement, from large-scale public architecture through to many utopian housing schemes, and private housing; revealing the many masterpieces created during this period. Among the numerous buildings featured are Mies van der Rohe's Seagram Building, New York, and Farnsworth House, Illinois; Mendelsohn and Chermayeff's Bexhill Pavilion, England; and Le Corbusier's Villa Savoye, Poissy, and Unité D'habitation, Marseilles, both in France. This lively and informative analysis of the subject covers key aspects of Modernism, including the art and culture of the period.

PB 1 85490 389 6
240 x 225mm, 68 pages
Illustrated throughout, mostly b/w
April 1996

Further information can be obtained from Academy Group Ltd, Tel: 0171 402 2141 Fax: 0171 723 9540, or from your local sales office:
VCH Publishers, 303 NW 12th Avenue, Deerfield Beach, Florida, Tel: (305) 428 5566 / (800) 367 8249 Fax: (305) 428 8201;
VCH, Boschstrasse 12, Postfach 101161, 69451 Weinheim, Federal Republic of Germany, Tel: 06201 606 144 Fax: 06201 606 184;
VCH, 8 Wellington Court, Wellington Street, Cambridge, CR1 1H2, Tel: 01223 321111 Fax: 01223 313321

FRANKFURT

Admission
Day Ticket   DM 20.00
Students   DM 13.00
5-Day Ticket   DM 40.00

Opening Hours
March 14 – 18, 1996
Thurs – Sun   11 am – 8 pm
Mon   11 am – 6 pm

Prospect 96
The international
exhibition of con-
temporary photography
at the Frankfurter
Kunstverein and
the Schirn Kunsthalle.
Concurrent with
Art Frankfurt

Special Exhibition
"The Social Eye"
Where artistic
photography
refers to society

Information
Telephone
(0 69) 75 75 - 66 64
Fax
(0 69) 75 75 - 66 74

Catalogue
Publication date
March 1996
Box Office price   DM 20.00
Mail Order price   DM 35.00
(incl. postage and
packing, payment by
crossed check)
Order from:
Messe Frankfurt
Service GmbH
Ludwig-Erhard-Anlage 1
60327 Frankfurt am Main
Germany

Visitor Academy
With guided tours,
lectures and dialogues
with artists

ART Frankfurt
The fair that keeps to the
subject of art

March 14 – 18, 1996

PUBLIC ART

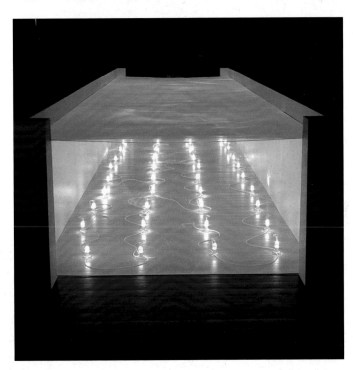

Matthew Dalziel and Louise Scullion, Sargassum, *1995*

Art & Design

PUBLIC ART

OPPOSITE: Christian Marclay, Amplification, 1995. Photo: Pierre Antoine Grisoni, CH-Morges; ABOVE:
Those Environmental Artists (TEA), Other People's Shoes, 'Life Style Choices', 1995. Photo: Paul Grundy

ACADEMY EDITIONS • LONDON

Acknowledgements

We would like to thank Amanda Crabtree for her dedication and commitment in putting together this issue of *Art & Design* and all the contributors for their generosity in providing material. Unless otherwise stated, all images are courtesy of the artist/s: **p28** © Locus + 1995; **p81** Office fédéral de la culture, Berne; **p85** *Burn Out* is represented by Gallery Nicolai Wallner, Copenhagen and Emmanuel Perrotin, Paris.

Amanda Crabtree works at Le Fresnoy, studio national des arts contemporains, a post-graduate school and contemporary art space to open in 1996 in the north of France. She has been researching public art for a number of years, has set up several public art projects in France and contributes to art journals in both Britain and France. **Judith Findlay** is a writer based in Aberdeen and Glasgow. She regularly contributes to *Flash Art International* and is a lecturer in History of Art and Contextual Studies at The Robert Gordon University in Aberdeen. **Matthew Dalziel** and **Louise Scullion** live and work in Scotland. Contributions to important projects and exhibitions include The British Art Show 1990 and General Release at the Venice Biennale 1995. They are preparing for a major solo exhibition at the CCA in Glasgow, Dec 95/Jan 96. **Susan Jones** is an artist who is also involved in undertaking visual arts research and consultancy. Since 1981 she has been a contributing editor to *Artist's Newsletter*. Recent published works include *Training of Visual Artists and Arts Administrators* with Lee Corner and David Patten, 1994 and *A Study of the Scope and Value of Artist-led Organisations,* 1994-ongoing. Former editor of *Public Art Review*, **Jeffrey Kastner** is a writer recently relocated to his native US after two years in Britain. Contributing editor to *Art Monthly* in London and a Boston Correspondent for *ARTnews*, his writings have appeared in numerous publications, including *Art & Design, Artforum, Frieze* and *Flash Art*. He is currently at work on *A Source Book: Land Art 1945-1995*, to be published by Phaidon Press, London, in 1996. **Mary Jane Jacob** is an independent curator based in Chicago who curated at the Museum of Contemporary Art in Chicago and at the MOCA Los Angeles, before realising several important public art projects in the United States. She is now a consultant to the Three Rivers Arts Festival in Pittsburgh and is also preparing a visual arts programme with the Arts Festival of Atlanta which will run concurrently with the 1996 Olympics. **Bruno Dupont** worked at the contemporary art centre Le Magasin in Grenoble before setting up the independent organisation @Art Connexion in Lille which realises projects with artists and sets up artists' residencies and exchange schemes. **Gilbert Boyer** is an artist based in Montreal, who has participated in international contemporary art exhibitions including 'Pour la suite du monde' and 'Art et espace public', and has carried out a number of public art commissions. He is currently working on public art projects in Vancouver and Valenciennes, France. **Valérie Mavidorakis** is an art historian living in Paris. She is currently writing a thesis on minimal art in the artistic theoretical and cultural context of the 1960s and 70s in the United States. She writes regularly on the subject of public art and contributes to *Parachute, Faces* and *Cahiers* of the Institut pour l'Art et la Ville. **Gérard Collin-Thiébaut** is a French artist who works on the representation of existing images in the form of stamps, stickers, tickets or puzzles. They are often distributed in the 'public' space for a 'new race of collectors'. **Mark Lewis** is an artist whose work has been exhibited internationally. In 1985 he co-founded the artists' and writers' collective Public Access; he is a founding member of *Public* and in 1994 he co-curated 'Queues, Rendezvous and Riots' at the Walter Phillips Gallery at the Banff Centre in Alberta. **Johanne Lamoureux** holds a professorship in the art history department at l'Université de Montréal. A founding member of La société d'esthétique du Québec, she has served on the board of several periodicals and is a regular contributor to a number of publications in North America. **Christian Marclay** lives and works in New York and has been involved in a number of solo and group exhibitions, including the Whitney Biennal in New York in 1991, he represented Switzerland in the Venice Biennale 1995. **Russell Ferguson** is Editor at the Museum of Contemporary Art, Los Angeles. Danish artists **Henrik Plenge Jacobsen** and **Jes Brinch** are based in Paris and Copenhagen respectively. They work both individually and together on exhibitions and performance and public art projects. **Miriam Rosen** writes for the French newspaper *Libération* on both public art and new technology.

Front Cover: Ann Hamilton, 'Indigo Blue', *Places with a Past*, Charleston, 1991. Photo: John McWilliams
Back Cover: Gilbert Boyer, *Voyettes*, Auby, 1995. Photo: Jean-Philippe Mattern
Inside Covers: Gilbert Boyer, *Cavalier noir*, Auby, 1995. Photo: Jean-Philippe Mattern

EDITOR: Nicola Kearton ASSISTANT EDITOR: Ramona Khambatta
ART EDITOR: Andrea Bettella CHIEF DESIGNER: Mario Bettella DESIGNER: Sonia Brooks-Fisher

First published in Great Britain in 1996 by *Art & Design* an imprint of
ACADEMY GROUP LTD, 42 LEINSTER GARDENS, LONDON W2 3AN
Member of the VCH Publishing Group
ISBN: 1 85490 230 X (UK)

Distributed to the trade in the United States of America by
NATIONAL BOOK NETWORK, INC, 4720 BOSTON WAY, LANHAM, MARYLAND 20706

Printed and bound in Italy

Contents

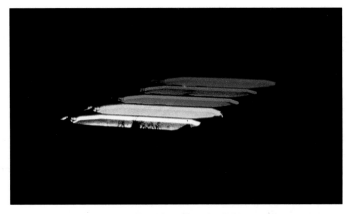

Jim Buckley, Flood, *1993*

ART & DESIGN PROFILE No 46

PUBLIC ART

Guest-Edited by Amanda Crabtree

Houston Conwill, Estella Conwill Majozo and Joseph de Pace, 'The New Charleston', Places with a Past: New Site Specific Art in Charleston, *1991, detail*

INTRODUCTION
Amanda Crabtree

Artists are not miracle workers – they're just another alternative.[1]

What do we mean by public space? Or the art within it? How can the two interact if the conditions are right? Misunderstanding related to the language of art in public spaces is no recent phenomenon. What this art should be and who it is destined for continues to provide the substance of endless reports and conferences world-wide on the theme of art and architecture.

One consequence of the current process of the transformation of the city environment and the questioning that accompanies it, is the increasing necessity to invent new models. The role of the artist in the urban space is being redefined and our expectations should be modified accordingly. This issue looks specifically at a selection of the current alternatives on offer.

Artists persist in inventing their own vocabulary, a language in which they modify the rules. Krzysztof Wodiczko and David Hammons established their artistic practice with a way of addressing the public which by-passes the monumental form, or the expectation of the public art *objet fixe*. Their commitment to the space of the city is defined in their use of pre-existing monuments or urban contexts as a basis for their work.

Judith Findlay and Valérie Mavidorakis offer examples of ways in which certain artists are currently working. This kind of art slips through the cracks of public spaces, asking questions, making you think but not necessarily coming up with the answers. It is not about making monuments but about making us see differently what is always in front of us. For it to function there should be something sufficiently different about it and notably that capacity to surprise, to jolt us out of our passive acceptance of normality.

Many of these projects often imply an ambiguity about the status and identity of such art. Judith Findlay asks artists Matthew Dalziel and Louise Scullion if they think art suffers because it is called art, suggesting that the danger of art announcing itself as art is the immediate exclusion of a category of people.

But advocating that such works do not have to be claimed as art, or special, does not infer that they must 'blend in' totally. These particular public art objects hover between art and what is exterior to the domain of art. Christian Marclay's installation in San Stae in Venice clearly shows that they can still be beautiful but they often show little concern for aesthetics. They may contribute to keeping alive the eternal 'But is it art?' debate and the unsettling *Burn Out* project in Copenhagen by Henrik Plenge Jacobsen and Jes Brinch is yet another example of this.

Questioning the public art object is fundamental in the 'Culture in Action' project led by Mary Jane Jacob in Chicago where the emphasis is moved away from objects and actions towards processes that create cultural activity, whether or not art is the final product. The basic concern is less for public space than the involvement of the community within which the work is placed.

This 'new genre' public art with the importance of process over product contrasts with other subtle, quirky or simply beautiful interventions in the public space. Yet common to both are notions of accessibility and communication in relation to 'the public'. The term 'accessibility' takes on a different meaning when applied to art, and that which is destined to be public, in particular, as opposed to the version kept in specialised contemporary art boxes. However, the margins between them are beginning to blur and artists are intervening in both spaces.

Gilbert Boyer's investigations into the way the contemporary art world functions have led him to intensify his research into the methods of communication in the public sphere. For him, the concept of accessibility is connected to the apprenticeship of language. This means both the literal reading of the work and the relationship between words and world and how place comes into existence through what the inhabitants say. Language and local environment interlock in projects that record memory of place.

Notions of accessibility and communication are totally reversed when it comes to virtual spaces, or as Vito Acconci puts it: 'Public space, in an electronic age, is space on the run'.[2] Recent communication technology offers further possibilities to artists and hence changes the 'public's' access and relationship to the artist and their work. Miriam Rosen has explored the network to investigate the way in which artists are appropriating Internet. It is significant that established 'public' artists are among the first to manipulate effectively the language and resources of this emerging public space.

What 'public' can mean, what public art could be , is currently being researched by Susan Jones, and the social and cultural ideas shaping today's public spaces are further explored by Mark Lewis and Johanne Lamoureux. This debate on the way artists can and should work in public and how the public is involved in that process is likely to continue but perhaps, as Mary Jane Jacob suggests in her discussion with Jeffrey Kastner, we should stop expecting artists to work miracles and start looking at how the alternatives they offer can become the norm.

Notes

1 See this issue, Mary Jane Jacob interviewed by Jeffrey Kastner.

2 'Public Space in a Private Time', *Critical Inquiry*, Vol 16/4, 1990.

THERE'S NOT MUCH ART THAT'S LIKE A GOOD STORY

Judith Findlay

One summer when I was small I saw a sign with an elephant on it. It was like a road sign for hazards of falling rocks, sharp inclines and low flying aircraft. I was on a car trip with my parents, my brother and our dog, making slow progress in our Morris Traveller on a remote road in the west of Scotland, so the sight of elephants was strange. I suppose someone had been there before us with a sign they had made earlier, or with a pot of paint and a brush to alter some unsuspecting deer or sheep or cow. You never know though . . .

It is like the cultural phenomenon of the road cone on a statue's head. Cones, which are used for sectioning off parts of roads for parking or maintenance, look like pointed white and orange hats, so there is a tradition of putting road cones, of varying sizes, on the heads of statues. Cones fall off or disappear, but generally they are put back. It is an efficient system. It makes you wonder if there is a department with a policy to do with access to road cones for all. After the pubs close at night teams of discreet, expert climbers, or task forces of people with step ladders, or people who are just very tall, employed by a Cones Council perhaps, patrol the town, keeping our monuments properly covered with orange and white cones. There is an Education Officer conducting guided tours, and you can pick up a leaflet if you want to, for interpretive purposes.

There are other signs around besides cones and signs of elephants. Some people know that a few of these are art, but many people do not and so, I imagine, view these art signs (called public art or art in the public sphere) in much the same way as other public signs (cones or elephants or whatever, and for all I know these might have been made by artists too). Not long ago for example, at the side of a busy flyover in Glasgow for everyone in a fast lane or traffic jam, was placed a tiny sign saying 'HELL'. In the corners of selected bedroom and living room windows of tenements around the city shone a neon sign saying 'SLUM'. For a period of time over Christmas 1994 it did a city-wide tour – Bentinck Street, Nithsdale Road, Hill Street, Golfhill Drive . . . Perhaps it is still travelling. A red neon dog appeared too on the roof of a closed-down tobacco factory. Now real dogs roam in its yard. The closure of the factory was a blow for the local community, so in a vacant gap site a light blue leisure centre made from a chipboard box was opened, and there is a rumour that a public toilet is soon to open as a bar called 'The Ship', because that is what the sign says.

My reason for talking about road cones, elephant signs and public art projects by David Shrigley, which is what *Hell*, *Slum*,

Guard Dog, *Leisure Centre* and *The Ship* are, is that I think these are a few of the things which you can trust to take you some place else. They are pieces of stories, evidence of narratives. They are proof that something has happened and they make you feel that something else could happen. The point is the 'followability' of the narrative, myth or journey which takes you, and followability is a criteria, or measure of value, which allows you infinite choices and changes.[1] Art, and especially public art, does not depend on rules of interpretation, meaning or expression. These are contextual and in the context of the public sphere they are up for grabs and art is like any other sign (like cones for instance, or a flyover that never gets finished, it stops in mid air with its metal rods hanging in space, and you make up the next bit). Roland Barthes says evaluation functions outside of the law: 'I shall not judge . . . according to the rules of interpretation, the constraints of style (anyway highly illusory) . . . (I shall not wax lyrical concerning the "rigour", the "brilliance", the "warmth", the "respect for what is written", etc), but according to the image . . . given me'.[2] So I want to look at some images given to me by eight artists I have chosen. They live in Scotland and I think are characteristic of a sensibility and way of working here. Scotland is not the only place they work, and although they work in a public context they are not only public artists. Most show work in galleries too (and Shrigley makes books of drawings as well). Each way of working, each project, energises the other. They work well outside the law. They have followability.

Glasgow, and it is night, about 10.00pm, and dark and raining. There is an underpass tunnel we have to negotiate to cross the motorway bypass. It is not a nice thought, people get mugged in underpasses. Tonight, though, something is different as people turning the corner into the tunnel would seem to indicate by their cries of surprise. For, on one night in May 1994, Peter McCaughey filled the tunnel with film, and his work, called *Tunnel Vision*, leaked day to night. The work was made by video-recording people walking through the tunnel on a wet and windy day. The next evening the recorded images were projected onto a screen hanging in the centre of the tunnel which people could walk through. That night a person was confronted with the tunnel in day time – a sort of *trompe l'oeil* with screen characters compounded by real people walking through beams of light and silver screen. They threw their shadows which could not be picked out from filmed silhouettes. We had to make a choice – continue our journey into film or turn back (to real life?) and find another route. It was like jumping into a movie, or into a song.

Sauchiehall Street is a street in Glasgow where a sign was placed on an old disused language school saying 'PRETTY VACANT'. The 'pretty' was pretty – pink, scripted and neon. 'Vacant' was made from different letters and different typefaces, some neon, some not. It was a work by James Thornhill called *Letter-Twocker (Six Sites: 4 Consonants/2 Vowels)* and as an art work I suppose it may have been a comment on art's content and status. Its counterpart, a gallery piece, ran the line, 'Wasteland'. (Public art is pretty vacant and in the gallery it is a wasteland?) The Sex Pistols meets TS Eliot. So does 'High' and 'Low'. That it was a work using letters and words on a former language school was a nice touch.

'(Un)Bounded' is also a sign by Thornhill called *Letter-Twocker (Various Sites: 5 Consonants/4 Vowels)*. It is still fixed in Hutcheson Street above other signs for wrestling and rock listings in a place where affluent Glaswegians park expensive cars to buy expensive clothes and eat expensive food. At night, in a doorway below the 'B', drug dealers do business ('B' for business). *Letter-Twocker* relates to TWOC which is a type of low slang and high legal terminology meaning to take without the owner's consent. Thornhill takes letters without consent from vacant buildings and puts them on other vacant buildings. He claims the right to vacancy. He collects letters, stores them in his house, and sometimes finds himself walking around carrying an 'A', or a 'B', or a 'C' . . . It is a deviant, graffiti version of Sesame Street. The Cookie Monster, Ernie and Bert travel the city putting up signs. Perhaps they put up cones too. .

Fitzwilliam Square in Dublin is a dignified square of Georgian architecture. It is a place of residence and business, of the day time variety carried out in offices and the night time variety carried out in streets – it is locally well known that by night it is a place for picking up. For a time in March 1995 it was also a place where pairs of flashing blue and yellow neon circles hung in every corner. The circles were a work by Jim Buckley called *Neon Installation*. Fixed to buildings attached to sills so that they hung high between second and third floor windows, the coloured circles (the only coloured lights in the square) blinked on and off, one after the other. There is a fine line between what is thought proper and what is not is not there – two sides of the same coin perhaps. I suppose it depends on time and place, and on who thinks they have a right to be there, and how and when and why. Who knows what is going on behind closed doors for example. The circles were like targets for marking or signalling, or eyes or spy holes for watching and seeing. Some residents and office people were concerned. They thought the circles might attract more of the wrong kind of attention, more of the wrong kind of business. The girls were delighted. They wanted red circles too. The square was very silent at night. It was like being in a Jean-Jacques Beineix film or in a dark living room watching TV in a blue light.

Slupsk is in the north of Poland at the edge of the Baltic Sea. Standing by a river is an old witches' tower with a weather vein on top. The tower was damaged in the war but it has now been rebuilt, one side made entirely of glass. From the outside you can clearly see the stairs rising up through the three floors to the attic. Buckley made a light tower, flooding each floor with light of different colour – blue, green, yellow, and way up top, red. If you walked around the tower to the other side you could just make out a small red skylight shining in the roof.

Meiho is in a mountainous region south of the Japanese Alps. There is a valley there with an abandoned fish farm which you can see below as you cross the bridge taking the road into town. The bridge spans a ravine and a white-water river. A great waterfall is the only unbroken sound. In the fish farm Buckley made a work called *Flood at Dusk*. He cleaned out seven of the overgrown tanks of vegetation, then washed and painted them white. He started up the water system which meant that water flowed once more through the tanks. He fixed a lighting system too, which ran off a generator for two hours each night at dusk. Like the tower, each tank was differently coloured by light – white, yellow, blue, green and red. The colour shone through, was captured and held in each tank by the water.

Flood was meant to be temporary, but it was so well liked by the local people (a cheer went up when it was first turned on) that the Town Council and local landowner chose to keep it and had it connected up to the street lighting supply so that *Flood* switched on and off, at dusk and dawn, by itself. Fish and water are important in Japanese life and the Japanese usually rebuild rather than restore. By changing a familiar place slightly, and contemplating and altering a common tendency, Buckley made a well known and everyday site special. The square, the tower and the fish farm were highlighted spaces in everyday life set aside. They were reminders of an ever present but hidden side of reality, offering pathways to a little bit of mystery and wonder.

In a prosperous suburb of Glasgow called Eastwood (Kenny Hunter, an artist and friend of mine, called it 'Glasgow's Beverly Hills'), there is a well loved park called Rouken Glen. The park has a boating pond, with islands of rhododendrons, and a tea room with seats outside for nice weather, an ice cream kiosk and a concrete jetty where rowing boats are moored for hire. In April 1995, one of those moored was a fluorescent yellow boat, with a transparent deck and glass oars. The boat, along with photographs and sound, was a work by Ruth Stirling called *Miracle*. Working with people of the local Asian and Jewish communities in Eastwood, Stirling made a work which explored cross-cultural life and time, and ponds (usually the centre of a park just as a square is the centre of a city) and parks (which is a city's response to nature; a pond is like a safe sea), and the traditions of boating. *Miracle* was a means of transport and transference. McCaughey let people walk through the surface and Stirling let people sail on it. To experience *Miracle* you had to get in the boat and row out and around the pond so you could see floating photographs and hear island-based sound of people speaking, explaining, telling and remembering. You could do this with the other boats but it was not the same. They had dull colours, peeling paint, wooden oars and no glass floor. The yellow boat was best. It was not exclusive however, for you hired it like the rest. If the yellow boat was out when it was your turn you had to pick another. The boat was loved, not for being art, but for being a beautiful boat. Perhaps that is art though.

There is a grand old beech tree in Rouken Glen Park too. It stands at the top of the glen, at the side of a path on a grassy patch beside some bushes and monkey puzzle trees. Matthew Dalziel and Louise Scullion suspended their film installation, *The Gifted Child* from this beech tree. As Stirling's boat floated on a pond, images floated under a tree.

The work was made by suspending a large sheet of glass by wires from a sturdy bough. In the centre of the glass was a large disc shape which had been sandblasted so it looked frosted. For three evenings at weekends this piece of frosted glass caught and held back-projected film – moving images of the raw sea spliced with footage of a synchronised swimmer in a pool. It was silent, there was no sound. As you stood in the dark in front of *The Gifted Child* you could see the frilly hat, the clipped nose, the exaggerated movements and smile, but pared down to the minimum it made you concentrate on the beauty of a physical routine. It was sensuous, athletic, compelling and powerful. It was a huge moon hung in the bushes, and, walking across the park at night you could see it floating way off in the distance with a group of tiny dark figures gathered around.

Dalziel and Scullion previously made another work about a swimmer and the sea called *The Bathers*. It was made of three bathing huts each with a slatted floor, wooden stool and clothes hook. Projected onto glass, on a small frosted circle, at the back of each hut, was an 8mm film on a loop showing a woman swimming through waves, a man running down sand dunes and seagulls flying across the sky. *The Bathers* reminded you of childhood holidays and home movies and French films like *Pauline at the Beach*. It looked like a facility from a 1920s lido. It joined past and present worlds, and worlds of fact and fiction so it was meant to be graceful, idealised.

The Gifted Child, on the other hand, was about hardship. Water can look beautiful and sparkling but it can also rob you of life. *The Gifted Child* mixed a chlorine pool and the discipline of the swimmer with an open sea where there are no rules and regulations. It mingled the cultivated and controlled nature in parks, green houses and gardens with something in nature which is unsettling and wild. It blended culture with nature and something artificial, with something which is real, but perhaps because of this, is unknown.

Looking after plants can be a lot like looking after art. You have to care for them, put them in the right light and space, make sure their temperature and moisture is right, share them with others. Sometimes plants and art are practically the same. In Edinburgh there is a Festival Theatre where Phil Power will plant a creeper. The theatre is a major venue in the centre of town, an impressive new building made from glass. The trouble is it sits right next to a bare, stone gable end which people can see as they walk by the

PAGE 8: Jim Buckley, Flood at Dusk, *Meiho, Japan, 1993, concrete tanks, water, paint, lights, each tank 2.5 x 7 x 1m; David Shrigley, Glasgow, FROM ABOVE:* Guard Dog, *1991, illuminated image of a dog on top of Wills Tobacco factory;* The Ship, *1991, facade of a disused public lavatory altered to become a public bar;* Hell, *1991, roadsign displayed on a motorway exit*

11

theatre or wait to buy tickets. It is a drab sight for such an exciting place. So Power will plant *Parenthenocissus* (*tricuspidata* or *quinquefolia*) commonly known as Virginia Creeper. The creeper is a familiar vine, thickly covering walls in urban districts. It has beautiful crimson, 'autumn' leaves, bluish-black or purple berries and tendrils with sticky tips which cling. It is often planted for show and is hardy enough to stand up to city pollution. It climbs and covers areas of walls up to 70 feet in height. Power's creeper will grow from the base of the gable and be trained up the wall and onto lights – cold cathode (commonly known as neon), cyberlight and LED graphic boards. These lights will change, respond to sounds in the theatre, to what is going on inside. What is going on inside will seep outside in the form of images and words – messages and rumours which may trigger a memory later on, give a person a sense of *déjà vu* in the way that a piece of music might, or a smell, or an image which stays on your retina, or in your head. Power's work makes the gable end like a living thing which tells stories. It enables a journey other than walking past. It represents an everyday elsewhere.

The M8 motorway links Edinburgh and Glasgow and stretches east-west though Scotland's Central Belt. A long journey is a completely different mind-set and it is not only walking that represents an everyday elsewhere, for cars are vehicles, metaphors for meditation, and driving is a transport between two types of attention, of a here and now, and an elsewhere. It is a metaphor for myth. It is a story. Three hundred miles, four hundred miles. You can narrate a journey, reading hoardings and notices, noting down number plates, counting types and colours of cars, indicating interesting landmarks and sights. Once on a sunny day driving on a motorway, Dalziel and Scullion could see into all the cars – afro hair, Jewish caps . . . There was a guy on a motorcycle with these airbrushed images of California on his fenders. Driving sometimes seems an issue of faith, an issue of culture, and the motorway is a strange democratic, multicultural space – so are motorway cafés. One of Dalziel and Scullion's friends, Michael, once drove into a motorway café late at night. There were Harley Davidsons parked outside, and inside, monks in brown habits playing Sega machines. Michael said it was weird (a weird zone). That is what motorways are like though, a strange road with strange cafés, where strange mixes of people come together.

Dalziel and Scullion's work, *The Horn*, is for people on a motorway but they will have to search for it. It looks like a tall, thin, steel horn, or speaker, or oval trumpet. It is shaped like a swan. Standing 18 metres high it will be sited near, and point towards, the M8. It has a mystery, like an Oracle or Madonna. You make a pilgrimage. A hundred thousand people go and The Black Madonna does not weep. Then one more person goes, The Black Madonna weeps and the myth is revived. *The Horn* will be fitted with recorded sound of music, of songs and voices speaking of thoughts and memories, pieces of daily life. These messages will be played randomly to passing traffic through speakers and by short wave radio about every 20 minutes which will give you ample time to drive through *The Horn's* range. Perhaps a sign will tell you that *The Horn* and its frequency are near. *The Horn's* tendency to speak will be like the Madonna's to cry. Sometimes it will say something, other times it will not. You might never get what *The Horn* is about even if you stood before it forever. Maybe it is like going to Lourdes, it is the journey that counts – the followability.

This sense of difference, and difficulty, might make *The Horn* sound, however, as if it is part of a separate sort of art practice – art *vs* life. But I have said that art signs in the public sphere are perceived much like other signs so I would like to leave *The Horn*, along with the other works I have talked about, as part of life and as part of popular culture (and is not all art part of that anyway?)

It is a well known tale, but just to tell it again: Adorno and Horkheimer use the myth of Odysseus and the Sirens to explain the struggle of art *vs* popular or mass culture (and they of course argue that never the twain shall meet).[3] To navigate past the Sirens whose seductive, beautiful song will surely lure sailors to disaster on the rocks (and make them forget to eat and wash and things like that), Odysseus has his men stick wax in their ears so they will concentrate on the job at hand. He ties himself to his mast, ordering his men not to release him. As top man he hears the beautiful song and sees the Sirens singing, putting on lipstick and blowing kisses, but he is not free and cannot do anything. His men keep working but they do not hear. It is a knotty tale and one near impossible to get out of. There is no chance of a conversation. There is no chance of art and other things exchanging ideas, or supporting, characterising and influencing each other sometimes in wonderful and unexpected ways. It assumes too that people are passive and do not know what is good for them which I do not feel comfortable with. These works are different and sometimes difficult, that is true. Access to their messages might be limited. Sometimes they might speak to us and sometimes they might not. Their messages and our responses will be ambiguous, meaning will depend on our active interpretations – on our making of meaning. This sounds like art. But it also sounds very much like a popular culture (think of when you buy a great record), meaning culture as a collective thing in its widest sense, as a whole way of living.

That is why these works are familiar, or similar, too. They are found on familiar channels, in familiar contexts and forms. They are like familiar architecture, of motorway lighting and pylons, of horns, of rowing boats, of witches' towers, of fish farms, of tunnels, of climbing creepers. Their myths are like familiar myths – of saints, seers, plants and foliage, rivers, bridges, towers, crop circles, glass vessels, beasts, witches, swans . . . They are like living things, and although they stand out and are cast as outsiders, they are outsiders which do alright in life or society or culture – sort of ugly ducklings or Forrest Gumps. These works are part of a popular culture which we share collectively, yet that is not to say that we do not respond to them individually. Like other forms of media they promise the fulfilment of desire even if you have to wait forever to get it. There is a desire to follow.

PAGE 12: Peter McCaughey,
Tunnel Vision, *Glasgow, 1994;*
FROM ABOVE: *James Thornhill,*
Letter-Twocker (Six Sites: 4
Consonants/2 Vowels), *Glasgow;*
David Shrigley, Slum, *1994, neon
displayed in various locations,
Glasgow*

Louise Scullion told me of a story by JD Salinger about a child far more intelligent than his years called 'Teddy'.[4] It is the story which influenced the title of *The Gifted Child*. Teddy has this theory about how people should spit out all the apples they have eaten in their lives. This would let them look at things afresh, with intuition. The apple is biblical, it comes from the tree of knowledge and Teddy believes that people have too much of a sort of knowledge which stops them from seeing things clearly.

Perhaps we need to spit out some 'Art' apples in order to see public art works clearly. Then we might be able to relate to them like other signs in our culture, on their own merits and not by the category of 'Art' (like signs of elephants, cones, half finished flyovers, music, film, perfume, food, clothes . . .)

Garrison Keillor tells about a young dad called Kenny who tells his kids the story of Hansel and Gretel. The story is familiar but it is hard to tell your kids who you love about a dad who abandons his children in the forest to be eaten by wolves. 'Kenny sometimes forgets a detail but his kids remember each one, and if the breadcrumbs on the path sparkle like diamonds in the moonlight in one version of the story, then the next time you can't say they glisten like pearls, you've got to tell it the same way. You can't disappoint them but you also have to surprise them, so each time

he'll toss in something new and crazy – maybe the gingerbread house will have a garage this time, made of pepperoni pizzas, and the wicked witch will sit drinking coffee and watching TV – but Kenny has to be careful: next time he can't say the pizzas were sausage and onion. Stories are permanent.'[5]

In stories there is a tension of repetition and novelty. Desire is kindled by things which are different and yet which in some way subtly innovate the life of the original seductions of stories which are similar or familiar.[6] Storytelling depends on context and no two tellings are ever the same. Storytelling is a way of finding meaning, magic, faith, wonder and mystery, for and through ourselves, in real life, a way of signalling something special in 'everydayness'. Perhaps these are reasons why stories are permanent even when the telling is temporary. Perhaps these are reasons why good public art works could be likened to pieces of stories. For while it is difficult to say what good art is, perhaps 'followability' could be a reading of value. In real life art works are not 'Art' but desirable signs of stories to be followed, fragments of narratives, routes waiting to be discovered. However, there is not much art that is like a good story, but some works, like familiar stories, are different. We can recognise stories, myths about us, which take us somewhere else. Where do you want to go today?

Notes

1 Paul Ricoeur, *Time and Narrative*, trans Kathleen McLaughlin and David Pellauer, 2 vols, University of Chicago Press, Chicago, 1984, Vol 1, p67.

2 Roland Barthes, *Image Music Text*, Fontana, London, 1984, pp188-189.

3 Theodor Adorno and Max Horkheimer, *Dialectic of Enlightenment*, Verso, London, 1944, p34.

4 JD Salinger, 'Teddy', *For Esme – With Love and Squalor*, New English Library, London, 1968, pp158-188.

5 Garrison Keiller, 'Hansel', *Leaving Home*, Faber and Faber, London, 1988, pp219-224.

6 See Georgina Born, 'Against Negation, for a Politics of Cultural Production: Adorno, Aesthetics, the Social', *Screen*, Vol 34, no 3 (Autumn 1993), pp223-242. She uses the example of 'the best mainstream pop'. See p232.

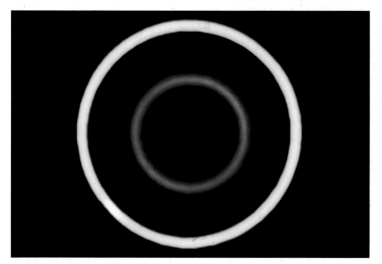 

Jim Buckley, L to R: Neon Installation, *Fitzwilliam Square, Dublin, 1995; Philip Power,* Computer Model, *Edinburgh Festival Theatre, 1995, red ivy, neon, computer simulation, electronic imaging*

FROM ABOVE: Television Cloth, *1994;* Television Cloths, *1994, photographed on St Combs beach*

things in this country: a management-led rather than practice-led approach. In short, the strategy rests on setting up specialist officers or agencies (with office space, administrative support, an accountable management structure and the right people on the board), devising suitable policies which dovetailed neatly into urban regeneration schemes, then going out to locate the artists who could perform the 'art' functions required by 'clients' (property developers, architects, local authority departments), many of whom might not know a lot about art (but, of course, knew what they liked when they saw it.) As many artists were new to the public art game and did not 'speak the lingo', the specialist officers or agents would be invaluable as mediators, smoothing the way and 'interpreting' between clients and artists.

Nowadays, however, there are an increasing number of examples of artists or groups of artists working in the public art sphere who prefer to do their own negotiation and mediation and take on the role of artist/consultant without any help from an agency or officer, taking an equal part within design teams in shaping decisions about a whole scheme rather than just the 'art works' sited there. It does seem, however, that the funding bodies find this practice-led approach more difficult to cope with because it does not fit into the neat structures they have devised. Furthermore, there is a strong possibility that a practice-led approach may generate different kinds of art than the administrators are expecting: temporary rather than permanent, live art rather than fine art, etc. In an arts system hide-bound by planning structures, accountability criteria, partnership funding and ever-changing policies, artists and their creativity can present real problems!

Notwithstanding that, artists working in the public art field are in an odd position professionally. They may be mistrusted by architects and planners, as reflected in a conversation between Philomena Davidson-Davis and Will Alsop: 'What do you think are the most successful collaborations between architects and sculptors?' 'Not sure I can think of any'.[5]

Furthermore, a fine art training still does not adequately cover the requirements of a public art practice, career structures are poorly defined and artists are badly rewarded in comparison with other design professionals.

Sara Selwood's book wonders why artists tend to be differently treated from other design professionals, that is, placed in a more privileged position and: ' . . . granted a higher degree of autonomy than other professionals. Why this should be the case, and why artists should be regarded as capable of serving wider interests than other professional groups is rarely questioned'.[6]

Colin Wilbourn, ABOVE and CENTRE: The Upper Room, *elm, sited near Prebends Bridge, Durham, 1988; BELOW:* The Red House, *July 1994*

NAME AMANDA

VENUE MUDS TOWN HALL

DATE 3/2/93

MEASURE?
PHOTO?
CASTS?
BOX A?
BOX B?
BOX C?
BOX D?

OTHER PEOPLE'S SHOES

AMANDA

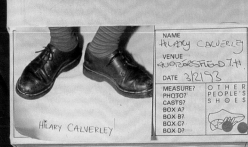

NAME HILARY CALVERLEY

VENUE HUDDERSFIELD T.H

DATE 3/2/93

MEASURE?
PHOTO?
CASTS?
BOX A?
BOX B?
BOX C?
BOX D?

OTHER PEOPLE'S SHOES

HILARY CALVERLEY

NAME NORRIS

VENUE BELMONT

DATE 18.2.93

MEASURE?
PHOTO?
CASTS?
BOX A?
BOX B?
BOX C?
BOX D?

OTHER PEOPLE'S SHOES

NORRIS

NAME ANTHONY

VENUE MECHANICS

DATE 17. FEB. 1993

MEASURE?
PHOTO?
CASTS?
BOX A?
BOX B?
BOX C?
BOX D?

OTHER PEOPLE'S SHOES

ANTHONY

NAME KAT

VENUE A.C. DEWSBURY

DATE 20.1.93

MEASURE?
PHOTO?
CASTS?
BOX A?
BOX B?
BOX C?

OTHER PEOPLE'S SHOES

KAT KATEZYVA
24, RISKA

NAME BARBARA GANGE

VENUE BELMONT CLUB

DATE 18/2/93

MEASURE?
PHOTO?
CASTS?
BOX A?
BOX B?
BOX C?
BOX D?

OTHER PEOPLE'S SHOES

BARBARA. GANGE.

NAME

VENUE

DATE

MEASURE?
PHOTO?
CASTS?
BOX A?
BOX B?
BOX C?
BOX D?

OTHER PEOPLE'S SHOES

TIM AUSTIN

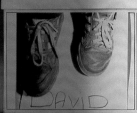

NAME David Parkinson

VENUE BUSY BEE Club

DATE 16 February

MEASURE?
PHOTO?
CASTS?
BOX A?
BOX B?
BOX C?
BOX D?

OTHER PEOPLE'S SHOES

DAVID

NAME KIM

VENUE BELMONT COMMUNITY CENTRE

DATE 18. 2. 93.

MEASURE?
PHOTO?
CASTS?
BOX A?
BOX B?
BOX C?
BOX D?

OTHER PEOPLE'S SHOES

KIM

NAME MAVIS WRIGHT

VENUE B B CLUB

DATE 16/2/93

MEASURE?
PHOTO?
CASTS?
BOX A?
BOX B?
BOX C?
BOX D?

OTHER PEOPLE'S SHOES

MAVIS WRIGHT

NAME LITTLE ALVIN

VENUE BELMONT CC.

DATE 18. 2. 93

MEASURE?
PHOTO?
CASTS?
BOX A?
BOX B?
BOX C?
BOX D?

OTHER PEOPLE'S SHOES

LITTLE ALVIN

NAME NURJAHAN BEGUM

VENUE CHIQUR ST.

DATE 17/2/93

MEASURE?
PHOTO?
CASTS?
BOX A?
BOX B?
BOX C?
BOX D?

OTHER PEOPLE'S SHOES

NURJAHAN

Those Environmental Artists (TEA), Other People's Shoes, *1992-94, OPPOSITE: 'Consumer Research Boxes'; ABOVE: 'Retail' – Lifestyle Choices.*
Photos: Jo Bradbury

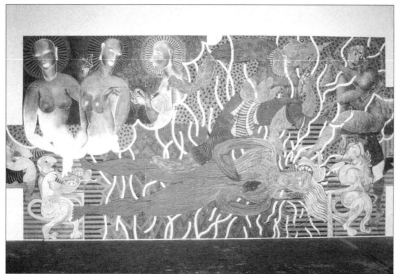

Locus +, FROM ABOVE: John Newling, Skeleton, *installation, All Saints Church, Newcastle-upon-Tyne, March 1994. Photo: Simon Herbert; Nhan Nguyen,* Temple of My Familiar, *mural, Blackstaff Mill, Belfast, September 1994. Photo: Jon Bewley; Stefan Gec,* Natural History, *photo-work for Pilgrim Street Fire Station, Newcastle-upon-Tyne, April 1995. Photo: John Kippin; OVERLEAF: Those Environmental Artists (TEA),* Other People's Shoes, *1992-94, 'Museum'. Photo: Paul Grundy*

AC: One conclusion of Selwood's *The Benefits of Public Art* is: 'Where appropriate, the commissioning of permanent works of public art – in particular by the public sector – should be subject to consultation'. When is it not appropriate to consult the public?

SJ: Sara Selwood's publication points to many of the woolly and misguided assumptions which have underpinned public art practice and in particular the inherent problems of putting 'art' and 'public' together. Amongst her case studies[7] are examples where a practice-led approach supersedes the sort of 'consultation' exercises usually undertaken within the administrator-led approach: public meetings, running workshops for local schools, putting maquettes in the library and asking people to vote on which ones they like best. In the revitalisation of Smethwick High Street, Francis Gomila 'spent the first twelve months developing contacts and relationships within the local authority'. He set up his studio within the community and during his first year, 'completed murals and mosaics and organised a street festival'. The emphasis was on communication, so that developing plans for repainting the shop fronts grew naturally from his relationship with the traders who became wholly committed to his proposal as a result. Commissions which develop from 'residency' type situations mean that 'consultation' is not something done at regulated intervals, but something which is a continuous, as the artists work on a daily basis.

The artist's personality has a lot to do with it too, and respect for the artist's work means neglect or vandalism is less likely. Two examples which spring to mind are Ken Watts's mural, painted on a gable end in the mid-70s in the east end of Sunderland which remained untouched by vandalism throughout its life, protected by the interests of local people in 'their mural', and Colin Wilbourn's *The Upper Room* sculpture sited in 1988 on the river bank below Durham Cathedral and carved during his year-long residency at the Cathedral.

AC: Is there any headway being made into the 'democratic process' which is supposed to save public art?

SJ: Firstly, I would like to make a comment about residencies and their role within public art. It is perhaps assumed that residencies and work which is more concerned with engagement than art-making *per se* are 'community art' and somehow a bit inferior to 'public art'. And whilst some public art projects are linked with residencies, because these are generally undertaken by artists not already living in the area, the community's involvement may be fairly superficial: workshops in a school for example, rather than an attempt at making any great in-roads into the local community as a whole. However, put simply, there may not be a need for 'consultation' in a public art project where it forms part of the work an artist does in his/her local community *because they live there*, and where the artist gains the respect of, and establishes a rapport with the people. US examples of artists whose work is inextricably tied to engagement with people over a long period include Suzanne Lacy and Mierle Laderman Ukeles. For example, Suzanne Lacy's fascinating *Crystal Quilt* project

(1987) is, according to Hafthor Yugvason ' . . . a classic prototype of an attempt to empower through participatory examination of values, prejudices and alternative visions. The success of such projects should not depend on whether the communities engaged will come to accept them – for without their active involvement from the beginning, the projects will not even get off the ground. Rather, the test is whether the art plays a real role in the participants' lives and leaves them with a fuller sense of their political and cultural power'.[8]

It is my view that this type of approach, of engagement and a long term aim, is far superior to any kind of 'consultation' or post-artwork mediation. A better way to describe it would perhaps be to think instead about how best to build audiences for visual arts in the long run. I think that artists, because they are part of their immediate community, play an important part in that process, and as a matter of course 'touch' many people with their art and their philosophies about its sphere of influence.

AC: What sort of structures are likely to be in place to support the visual arts in, say, ten years time?

SJ: The public art agencies grew up at a specific time and in response to a specific set of circumstances. I would hope that in time this rather rigid structure would give way to something more organic so that a range of methods are available to create interaction between artists and others. There should be, in future, far more room for artists to work directly with commissioners and architects. The philosophy behind the setting up of a National Artists' Register by AXIS (a visual arts information service) was to enable such contacts to happen more naturally. A commissioner should be able to use this multimedia facility – eventually from a terminal anywhere in the UK – and call up images and information accordingly.

Unlike the Labour Party, however, I am not too convinced about a stronger role for local authorities nor their reliance on public art/per cent for art policies as saviours of the visual arts. Mark Fisher, the Shadow Arts Minister stated: 'Central government spends over £5 billion a year on buildings and renovating existing ones. With the Millennium Fund, National Lotteries and the pent-up demand for new buildings, this figure is likely to rise. In developing a public art/per cent for art policy tied to building work, the potential for government to give a positive lead in support of visual arts is obvious . . . A strong lead from central government should act as encouragement to more local authorities. It is these authorities whose arts policies will be strengthened by a new statutory responsibility who can have the greatest impact on local artists, by developing new exhibition spaces, commissions, educational work . . . '[9]

But although *in theory* these authorities have the potential for delivering good art policies and enabling public art work, there are many examples of political expedience taking precedence over any meaningful long term planning. To put it bluntly, there is an awful lot of parochialism in local government, which could

cause a great deal of innovative work – the sort of work that stimulates and rejuvenates visual arts – to fall through the cracks.

AC: What are the conclusions so far of your research into the scope and value of artist-led organisations?

SJ: Around 17 per cent of these are likely to be involved in work which covers community action, public art or environmental work, with most of them not making permanently-sited works. Although I have yet to do the detailed case studies, I can already identify some whose work seems to be stretching the existing boundaries. Organisations such as TEA (Those Environmental Artists) seem, in my view, not to be at all concerned with what Graham Roberts of the Yorkshire-based agency Public Arts described in 1993 as 'playing games with those controlling the regenerative forces'.[10] Rather, they are concerned with ' . . . creating art works which take as their starting point the world as we find it. Our work is a form of research which questions the nature of the built environment and material culture that surrounds us. We conduct our enquiries by setting up temporary institutions which parallel and interact with the systems of society. These provide a host or framework for collecting, processing and presenting data and enable other people – specialists, other artists, the public – to contribute'.[11]

Artist Ian Hunter, a radical thinker and co-founder of Projects Environment is a key person in current debate about where visual arts practice might be heading. In recent years, Projects Environment has organised a series of seminars and conferences with an international scope on topics such as landscape and art, art and the urban environment and, in 1994, one which looked at 'new zones in critical practice'. His interest 'is in how the emerging tradition of artist-led initiatives is likely to reveal clues about the way forward for artists, and the possibility of locating creative/ critical practice beyond the remit of the art world . . . Look again . . . and I think you will see that they not only seek to operate in new zones outside the art world, but more importantly, they are about devising new methodologies in practice, most of which have little or nothing to do with what we now understand as mainstream visual arts practice'.[12]

And although my research shows that not all artist-led organisations are innovative or exemplary, some definitely do provide those stimulating examples which are needed to feed the development of visual arts. How such work can be financially enabled within an arts system which is hide-bound by public accountability and management structures is a moot point. Practice-led approaches have never fitted neatly into those well-defined planning structures: there are fewer and fewer opportunities for arts funders to 'respond' to artists' ideas, and more and more reliance on 'strategic planning'.

In such a climate, it is difficult to see how much scope (in funding terms) there will be for the development and support of artist-led/practice-led approaches. However, whether artists regard arts funders as their main source of support is debatable. In the UK, the awards to artists' schemes have diminished over the years, and many artists now choose to support their work through a variety of methods: teaching, consultancy, critical writing, community arts projects, etc, as well as through arts or non-arts related work. This approach has been described as a 'portfolio career', and one in which there is potential for artists to exercise a greater degree of control over whom and how they work. Because artist-led organisations are organic they may not last long or may quickly change from one 'animal' to another, essentially because they are practice rather than funding-led. Irish artist Eilis O'Baioll, commented: 'Funding bodies may never fully understand or support [artists whose work is concerned with social issues] . . . but [because] for the [artists] social intervention rather than financial gain is the ultimate objective', it may never be realistic for artist-led organisations to expect to be supported through traditional funding structures.[13]

AC: Is the gulf between public art and the curator/mainstream gallery system still as noticeable?

SJ: Because of the growth of 'exhibitions/public art/performances' talking place outside galleries (or perhaps artists' desire to recreate galleries in other types of space) – I am thinking of the work of (the now defunct) Edge, Locus +, Fine Rats International, Space Explorations, etc – and of the growing trend for artist-curators, the gulf between public art as it has been and gallery practice will inevitably lessen.

Work like Stefan Gec's *Natural History* seems to work on a number of levels. This marked the nine-year anniversary of the Chernobyl disaster and was developed by the artist – a second-generation Ukrainian – and the artist-led organisation Locus +. The three-stage project began with the temporary siting in April/ May 1995 on the roof of Newcastle Fire Station of portraits of the first six firefighters to lose their lives when Chernobyl exploded. This event took place largely because of the enthusiasm of Tyne and Wear Fire Brigade who saw involvement with the project as a development of a relationship between themselves and firefighters in Kiev which had existed since the disaster occurred. They had raised funds for the international appeal and later sent firefighters over. For them, *Natural History* was a valuable way to raise their profile in the community, and the Chief Fire Officer had no problem either discussing this 'art' project on BBC Radio's Kaleidoscope programme. At a later date Gec went to the Ukraine to produce a photo/textual diary about Chernobyl's aftermath, and the project was subsequently represented as an exhibition in Derry's Orchard Gallery in September of 1995.

Other People's Shoes was a collaboration between Those Environmental Artists (TEA) and the Impossible Theatre Company. Although it was part-funded by the Arts Council through their New Collaborations scheme, it also had to reach out beyond such traditional art structures if it was to fulfil the artists' intentions. The starting point was the humble shoe, and the project 'an investigation of an everyday object . . . [which is] the tip of the iceberg, visible but not seen. Out of sight and often out of mind

Those Environmental Artists (TEA), FROM ABOVE: Anxiety and Escapism, *1994. Photo: Paul Grundy;* Living Space, *Upper Campfield market, Manchester, 1991*

behind a reflective glass façade are the national and multinational companies managing and structuring the economies and cultures of the countries in which they operate. A vast production network . . . bringing us not one shoe but millions of the same shoe . . . a manufactured myth called freedom of choice . . . [this] was an attempt to temporarily invert the iceberg and maintain a delicate balancing act, examining the complexities of the industrial network, mirroring certain aspects to formulate an artwork'.

The artists were concerned to make a real cross-fertilisation between art and industry with the project. Taking place over an 18-month period, the stages of the project were described using industrial terminology: consumer research, design, production, distribution, retail and museum. 'Activities' took place in many places including industrial shoe design workshops, empty high-street retail outlets, colleges, artists' own studios, and also in galleries. And although it worked as a concept, the test would be whether it also worked as a 'live' project. But the clear plan and organisational structure ensured that over the lengthy running period – which took place in the North West, Midlands and Yorkshire – it maintained its intellectual rigour, becoming neither self-indulgent nor allowing the artists to be seduced by 'art world' endorsement of the installations themselves. Hundreds of people were involved along the way, with each stage attracting attention: local papers to national arts press; even the BBC World Service covered it.

Notes

1 Quotes from *Art in Public*, AN Publications, 1992.

2 Transcript of the conference 'Public Art – the New Agenda, University of Westminster, 1993.

3 *Public Art Review*, issue 9, 1993.

4 *Public Art: A Review*, Arts Council of Great Britain, 1991.

5 *Sculpture*, RBS, issue 1, 1995.

6 *The Benefits of Public Art*, Sara Selwood, PSI, 1995.

7 *ibid.*

8 Hafthor Yugvason, *Public Art Review*, issue 8, 1993.

9 *Artists' Newsletter*, August 1995.

10 Transcript from New Voices in the City: Art and the Urban Environment Conference, 1993.

11 *Refreshing Alternatives*, Stage 1 of a study of the scope and value of artist-led organisations by Susan Jones, 1995.

12 *ibid.*

13 *Artists' Newsletter*, July 1995.

Fine Rats International, OPPOSITE: Francis Gomila, 'Jump Fucker, Jump', 35mm projection at Out of Order, 1992; ABOVE: Ivan Smith, 'Burial', sculpture at Un-Earth, 1995

MARY JANE JACOB

An interview with Jeffrey Kastner

The paradigmatic shifts which occur from time to time within disciplines are slow to materialise and often the natural evolutionary result of subtle, broadly-based changes. Yet there is frequently a single individual who takes the first steps, someone whose work makes possible the initial move away from established conventions towards a new way of thinking about a particular cultural mode. In the realm of art for public spaces – a field of artmaking which has often seemed hopelessly mired in bureaucratic minutiae, curiously adrift from the kinds of vital theoretical debates which have invigorated other areas of contemporary practice – the last several years have seen a quiet but nonetheless important re-evaluation of both means and ends; a shift in the way of thinking about, if not always executing, public art projects.

Mary Jane Jacob, an independent curator based in Chicago, has been instrumental in working to develop new models for the conceptual formation and practical realisation of public art projects in the United States. Her two most recent major projects – 'Places with a Past' for the 1991 Spoleto Festival in Charleston, South Carolina and the 1993 Chicago project, 'Culture in Action' – have set precedents in both professionalism of approach and conceptual creativity. The work included in both of these projects has, in its own way, reanimated discourse about issues essential to art for public spaces, issues which, while absolutely integral to the theoretical progress of the genre, had been under-examined in most debates about the direction of public artmaking and exhibition – namely the relationship of art to its socio-cultural and historical setting and the interface between artist, community and audience.

Raised outside New York City, the 43-year-old Jacob studied in Florida and Florence before receiving her MA from the University of Michigan in 1976. After a stint at the Detroit Institute of Arts, Jacob became Chief Curator at the Museum of Contemporary Art in Chicago in 1980, at the age of 28, where she organised exhibitions of artists including Magdalena Abakanowicz, Alice Aycock, Rebecca Horn, Gordon Matta-Clark, Robert Morris and Jannis Kounellis. In 1986 she left Chicago to take up the position of Chief Curator at the Museum of Contemporary Art in Los Angeles. During her time at MOCA, she produced shows by such artists as Christian Boltanski, Nancy Spero, Ann Hamilton, Richard Deacon, Mario Merz and John Baldessari, as well as the landmark 'A Forest of Signs: Art in the Crisis of Representation', in 1989.

Jacob left MOCA in 1990, after being approached by the Spoleto Festival USA and subsequently curated 'Places with a Past: New Site Specific Art in Charleston', an exhibition of 18 site-specific installations in historic locations throughout the city. The show, which featured pieces by artists including Chris Burden, James Coleman, Ronald Jones, Kate Ericson and Mel Ziegler and David Hammons, managed to unite an uncommonly high level of conceptual and formal execution usually found in museum installations alone, with the kind of site- and history-specific contextualisation that only art in public spaces can offer.

Yet if 'Places with a Past' represented a certain bellwether for the curation of art in public space, Jacob's next major project embodied an even more striking set of practical and theoretical considerations. 'Culture in Action', a two-year process of artists working in direct partnership with community members in Chicago, challenged virtually every convention of typical public art procedure – disrupting the distance between practitioner and audience by making the work fully dependent on the active participation of the community; opting for a model in which product did not always necessarily follow process; favouring open questions over easy answers. From a hydroponic garden that produced vegetables for local AIDS patients and an inner-city ecological station to an eponymously-titled candy bar produced by artists and local factory workers, 'Culture in Action' transgressed boundaries of maker and audience, of object and gesture, of art and society.

Now based in Chicago, Jacob is currently involved in a number of long-term projects which will come to fruition over the next several years. A consultant to the Three Rivers Arts Festival in Pittsburgh, she is co-ordinating a public art project for the summer of 1996 which will again bring artists and community members together. As consulting curator for the Fabric Workshop and Museum in Philadelphia, she is creating a series of artists projects which will tour domestically and internationally in different forms during the end of the decade, and is also preparing a visual arts programme with the Arts Festival of Atlanta which will run concurrently with the 1996 Olympics.

This interview is excerpted from two extended telephone conversations held between Jacob and myself during the first week of August 1995.

Jeffrey Kastner: Was art an important part of your childhood?
Mary Jane Jacob: It was not something particularly important in my family, but it was definitely present and quite integrated through the public school system. So there was contact [as a student] not only with the constant presence of art, but also with teachers who had come through a fairly sophisticated route and felt that cultural learning through museums was important. For example, to me the Museum of Modern Art was a place I liked a lot, without any

stigma – it was really easy for me to go by myself or with a friend because it was just a couple of stops away from my house on the E train. Having that possibility with regularity and normality was really quite significant. It seemed art was something that was available to every child and I was able to take advantage of it, as did many others.

JK: So when it became time to choose a college, was art still your main interest?

MJJ: Well, art was still this thing which I was gravitating towards. But then I had what I felt was the tragic blow from my parents at the point that I was graduating from high school. They chose to escape the urban problems of the late 1960s in New York and moved to northern Florida, which was sort of like going to hell for a 17 year old. The short story is that my undergraduate work ended up being at the University of Florida. I started in the art school, but there was also a very strong humanities based, general studies programme. And luckily, during that year, I discovered a programme which the University of Florida was affiliated with in Florence, and so my entire sophomore year was spent in preparation for spending my junior year in Italy. We can say that the four years as an undergraduate was spent going into and out of Italy. It was there I understood for the first time what an art historian was, what a scholar was and I thought, 'OK, I'll be a scholar'. I had really come to the art through the museum, though, not through the study – certainly not through the art class I had encountered in Gainesville as a college freshman. So, I thought the museum was the way I wanted to pursue being an art historian – not in a straight academic fashion.

Also I had gone through the painful experience of being in northern Florida, apparently without the cultural resources my grade school had offered. But they were nonetheless there, if very different. It took a whole lot more ferreting out and opening up my mind, which was important for looking at what was a possible way of conceiving cultural experiences – whether folk art, naive art or another kind of sort of general atmospheric cultural climate. This was an attitude I wanted to adopt and I did at least come to perceive what was around me in northern Florida during my undergraduate years. I finally came to learn from the experience, both locally as well as in high-culture Florence.

There was something even more significant about this Florence experience – not just that it turned me on to the notion of what a scholar could be or how that could be channelled through a museum route, but, more importantly, it was the way that one learned about art in Florence. I had not quite recognised it until just a few years ago when the *Places of the Past* book came out. I had sent one to Fred Licht (director of the Florence programme), with whom I still keep in touch. He wrote back and said he hoped that in some small way he had had an effect that had contributed to this achievement. I thought about it and wrote back to him and said, 'you know, as I think about how we learned about art in Florence, it was not only that there were museums there like the

Uffizi that one could go to and learn from, but everything that we did – the way that we came to know the city, looking at its medieval or its Renaissance plan, seeing the way the architecture works through the whole of the place – everything was really this totality and spoke to a larger meaning of how this art worked formally and conceptually within its physical setting and also spiritually within the life of people that were there'.

JK: A more synthetic approach that did not take the work out of its context?

MJJ: In Florence there was a real possibility of thinking about how art had meaning within context. That was not the issue when I was growing up in New York nor would it have been had I stayed there. If all museums were like MoMA, then I would not be doing what I am doing; I might not even be in the museum field. The kind of thing that we are involved in – bringing art to people, making greater communication vehicles, opening up the possibility of contemporary art within contemporary life – seems to be irrelevant when you are walking among the crowds at MoMA. You know, 'What's the problem? There're a lot of people'. If I had [stayed in New York] I probably would not have seen [the situation] any differently. There is plenty of audience. But this exists virtually nowhere else in the country for contemporary art.

So there is something terribly wrong and problematic about the intersection of art and audience at other museums outside that small circle of New York. That is why it was probably a good thing to go, at that pivotal point of 17 years of age, to a place like northern Florida, not to live there forever, but to cope with it; to understand that it had its own virtues. Then also to have the experience of a magnificent, let us say highest moment of Western Art, to be able to draw associations and parallels between Renaissance Italy and my own period in New York and in the kind of rural urban complex of a place like northern Florida. What it told me was that I wanted to go into art history, I wanted to follow that route through museums, and I also wanted to leave Florida and return to the north but not necessarily back to New York, because just like the study of Renaissance art did not need me, New York did not need me. And so it was fortuitous to take up the offer that was best, which was at the University of Michigan, and to go to Ann Arbor for graduate studies.

I worked in 19th- and early 20th-century American art and what was interesting about that programme which fits into what I was trying to express about Florence and how this dovetails back to some of my current work is that there, American art was taught and studied between the Art History and the American Culture programmes; it was art in context. So I was picking up on this interest in how art emanates from a place – which could be wood sculpture in rural northern Florida or the art of the Cinquecento in Florence: whatever your environment provides.

JK: So how did your graduate studies influence your choice of profession?

MJJ: Well, part of my dual programme in art history and museum studies was this important option to do an internship, but because the internship I wanted [at the Detroit Institute of Arts] would not have been available until the following year, I took up an additional opportunity with a programme called the Michigan ArtTrain.

JK: A train with art on it?

MJJ: Yes, it began in the early 70s and ended about 20 years later. It was a six-car train converted into galleries which was pulled across the country through the generosity of railroads. It was a didactic programme which took one very briefly from ancient art to the 19th century through the first few cars. Then there was one car entirely devoted to contemporary art, and the last car had three craftspeople at work, artists who were part of the staff that toured around.

The programmatic aspect of the Michigan ArtTrain which I would like to emphasise is that it was successful because the staff went into these communities a year ahead of time and began with educational programmes, with people preparing for the train to come, which eventually became like a one-week arts festival, a sort of celebration. But if the train had just pulled into town one day, none of that celebration could have been mobilised, nor would it have had any meaning for the public. So the whole concept of working within communities with the art prior to coming in was as important a lesson, maybe more, than any other of my graduate studies. Now we can come back to the ArtTrain and talk about its relationship to the late 60s or early 70s idea of bringing art to the people. But in the crescendo of my museum career at the end of the 80s, it was clear that we had exchanged this notion of bringing art to the people for the idea of art for the masses. I was interested in a democratic point of view, making art available to the broad public, not the marketing orientation of the blockbuster to bring in a mass audience. I was interested in bringing art to the people, but not art for the masses. By that I do not mean art has to be for a few people. I do not see the function of the museum as being that different from public art – they both have the goal of reaching the public. Yet, I think we have at times lost track of our reasons for bringing art to the public and that is not because people in the museums do not know what they are doing, but the pressures on them are very different today. When I think back to the time I spent in Detroit, my early exhibitions focused on Detroit artists and were also a means of becoming more philosophically enmeshed in the issues which were so much a part of what American contemporary art was all about at that time: the viability of making art outside the New York mainstream. I saw these exhibitions as a way of building bridges from the outside to the inside, so that one did not have to go out, but could make a place from within.

And then when I moved to Chicago in 1980, we were starting to open up to a more international world and I saw an example of the same kind of prejudice that we had experienced [in thinking about American regionalism] transferred to issues of the US *vs*

PAGE 36: Barbara Steinman, Ballroom, *'Places with a Past', Charleston, 1991; FROM ABOVE: Inigo Manglano-Oralle and Street-level Video, Tele-Vecindario; Simon Grennan, Christopher Sperandio and the Bakery, Confectionery and Tobacco Workers' International Union of America local no 552,* We Got It! The Workforce Makes the Candy of Their Dreams, *1993; OVERLEAF: Ann Hamilton,* Indigo Blue, *detail, 'Places with a Past', Charleston, 1991. Photos: John McWilliams*

the rest of the world. So one would ask, 'could there really be any good contemporary art in Europe, or if there is in Germany and Italy, certainly there's nothing interesting happening in France', and on and on. And I remember going to MOCA [in Los Angeles] in the mid-80s and people saying 'there really isn't any contemporary Japanese art'. These things sound so ridiculous and narrow-minded now, but the art world has a very fixed mentality of what is important art and what is not.

JK: Was a certain level of disillusion starting to develop with the institutional approach by this time?

MJJ: Well, there was disillusionment about what the institution could do for me in terms of my curatorial interests and if my curatorial direction could fit into the institution.

JK: You have talked about the feeling that you have had that there was a necessity to locate interesting art outside New York. I am wondering if you began to feel that not only did you want to leave the centre to do your work in a different institution, but perhaps you might leave the institution to do your work again on another level of independence from that.

MJJ: First of all, I do not want all the museums to blow up, or all of them to go away, so I am not anarchistic in that sense. Do institutions sometimes need to re-invent themselves? Do they need to move and change? Yes, everything does. Do things really need to change in terms of demographics and rethinking who lives in this country? Yes, and to try to make those issues of institutional survival and relevance a positive development, not just a matter of coping. Do I think that things can happen outside the institution? Yes. Florence is not an institution; it is a city and art is part of the life of the city. Do I like that kind of normalcy and the way that art can be a part of everyday life? Yes, and whether you are a shopkeeper or a curator or a citizen in Florence, it works in the same way.

JK: In terms of your professional approach, though, was it becoming clear to you that the work you really wanted to do might be better done outside the specific aegis of an institution like the museum?

MJJ: I felt that what I was doing spoke both inside and outside the institution. I still describe myself as a museum curator working outside the museum.

JK: Did you previously have a desire to curate museum exhibitions outside the museum, but found it impossible?

MJJ: It was an interest, and I had begun working in this way in Chicago because the Museum of Contemporary Art was so small. An important experience there was working with Jannis Kounellis on a major retrospective. This was work which needed air, and despite taking over the entire museum, we still did not have enough space, so I suggested acquiring another building and Jannis took on that challenge as something much more conceptual and integral to his work. He decided that he wanted four buildings, not one. And out of this he created not only a geographic map,

which became the tour of the exhibition, but a map by which he used these turn-of-the-century industrial buildings to tell a story of the passage from the old world to the new, from the 19th century to the 20th century, from Europe to the United States, through the metaphor of the immigrant. And so the whole city became involved in this story. So yes, I was always looking to go out into the street.

JK: You talked before about the notion of critiquing the institution and I imagined that is not something that one can do very well from inside the institution. Did you feel like the institution needed to be critiqued?

MJJ: Well, thinking critically about the institution, about its history, about what it presented or what it could present, is something I always thought about with every job and the particulars of that institution – be it Detroit or Chicago or Los Angeles. Critiquing the institution with a capital 'I' is also something that I think is of interest. But [it is not always immediately clear where a certain project stands] in relation to the institution. Although the Spoleto exhibition, for instance, which you have referred to as public art, happened outside the museum convention, had no admission and was inaccessible, I never thought of it within that vocabulary of public art. They were really installations that were driven by context and physical space. They were artists' installations which were neither driven by a public agenda nor seeking to enlist the local public to any great degree. And, like in a museum, we tried to get people to visit the sites; except for a few examples, it was not just there when you walked down the street.

JK: So your definition of 'public art' starts with a kind of real-time involvement with the community – it is not about being in public space as much as it is about involving the community within which the work is placed?

MJJ: Yes, and I would apply that same definition to the museum. A museum is not a dislocated thing: you are either in New York or Chicago or Minneapolis or wherever. You are part of that place. In a number of different ways you are part of that community: you are dependent on museums for membership, for funding, and you have a responsibility to teach the children. Furthermore, museums are community institutions as well.

JK: Yet museum shows do not usually address an issue of coming to some kind of compact with the community. There is a shift in there somewhere – from making a decision, as an expert in the field, about what is good for the community to what one comes to an agreement with the community about in terms of 'public art'. When you talk about public art, you seem to be talking about a thing which is executed with agreement. This dealing with the community in a kind of front end way is something that your work as a curator in public art has addressed in large part.

MJJ: I will not say this authority is democratically dealt with, so it still may be a kind of giving direction. Negotiating may at times be a way of gaining consensus or of being granted permission. When we sent works of art around in the ArtTrain, we did not ask people what they would like to see, we just picked it. But we did ask them to give it a chance and we brought them into the process of shaping how art could be part of their lives.

JK: There is something in that – one of the differences between Spoleto and 'Culture in Action' is the degree to which the work emerges from the community as a matter of fact. In 'Places with a Past', a lot of the works dealt with the social, historical and cultural context in a way that addressed the issue of a community. It seems, though, that 'Culture in Action' is a case of the work being in some ways entirely dependent on the activity of the community. So is there a more complicated shift between the audience and the artist that went on in Chicago than had gone on at 'Places of the Past'?

MJJ: Well, ironically, while 'Culture in Action' depended on the activity of the community, that community was in some ways less local than the Charleston community. 'Places with a Past' was very particularised in [its relationship] to the history of Charleston. It was very much of the past, and more about places than it was about people; whereas in Chicago the exhibition was fixed in a particular physical locale. The discussions that were going on could be replicated almost anywhere else because we were talking about AIDS, we were talking about housing, and while it is different when you are dealing with different individuals or a different town, the issues in Chicago were certainly not foreign to other places in the United States or other places in the world. 'Culture in Action' was more particular because of the actual individuals involved and yet more generally applicable and emblematic.

JK: There is another shift that occurred between Charleston and Chicago – away from objects and towards activities, towards process. Whilst you can still see the traces of the museum notion of creating an object and putting it in a place where people can experience it in Charleston, in Chicago it seems that less emphasis was placed on creating an artefact in a traditional sense, and more on exposing and challenging the processes that create cultural activity, whether or not they create art as an object. Do you think that one of the main reasons why some people found 'Culture in Action' so difficult to understand was its failure to produce objects which people could fit into the parameters they use to judge the quality of art?

MJJ: That was an issue for a large segment of the population. But I thought we had to go out to the extreme edge, not just to be provocative and weird but because I felt – like any show I have done – that it was a way of following what current trends in art were about. I did not invent or tell these artists to make this kind of work. This type of activity was already happening; I just drew a frame around it.

JK: But it does create a sort of interpretive comfort zone to have a

Daniel J Martinez and The West Side three-point Marchers, Consequences of a Gesture/100 Victories = 10,000 Tears, *'Culture in Action', Chicago, 1993. Photos: John McWilliams*

FROM ABOVE: David Hammons, America Street, *'Places with a Past'*, Charleston, 1991. Photo: John McWilliams; Chris Burden with The Fabric Workshop, Philadelphia, LAPD Uniform, 1994, installation view, wool serge, metal, leather, wood and plastic, uniforms: 88 x 72 x 6cm each, edition of 30. Photo: Will Brown

thing to look at and when that thing is not produced I think people find it difficult to follow it through.

MJJ: I think 'Culture in Action' was about the question of whether we need to have the object or not. And as for the public art objects that we do have, why do we have them, what meaning do they have for us and how can we look at them with new eyes?

JK: So you are not necessarily critiquing the object by promoting work which fails to produce it?

MJJ: Questioning it. Questioning whether that is the way to work right now; whether those objects that we already have still have meaning. I think for a lot of people public art is invisible: 'I don't even see it any more – I used to hate it, now I don't even see it'. So I wanted to reconsider the art which is placed in front of the public and also to ask if artists still need to make objects now. Or are there also other ways of making art, ie the non-object, which has a legacy in art history and can have a great deal of meaning and power in the present. Having grown up on avant-garde art and accepting it within a historical framework, I cannot understand the reactionary attitude of our critical community that says that this kind of work is not art. We can talk about how it fits in or how we understand it, but to scream that it is not art is surprising.

JK: I think for many people the problem is that they cannot put enough historical perspective between themselves and the work to see it as being a kind of cultural comment because it is still too alive as a social issue.

MJJ: Yes, it is not just that they cannot see it within a succession of styles, but because this work also critiques some other aspects of how our art world is constructed, challenging a kind of mainstream attitude that is based on privilege.

JK: I also get the impression sometimes that people feel it looks too easy, that it fails to step away from the mass culture sufficiently to make it seem like big, impressive ART. Because it is not about things we are familiar with in an artistic context – paintings and sculptures of kings and saints – people are suspicious of it.

MJJ: I would say absolutely that the biggest problem for some people in the art world is that others, outside, can get it in ways that are as right on as theirs, in spite of distances in education and art experience. They are drawing on life experience. This art can really talk across boundaries. Therefore, if you have worked all your life to have made the money to be able to acquire art, to have a kind of lifestyle and then somebody just comes in off the street and gets contemporary art too, you have lost all your cachet. I still keep a letter from a curatorial colleague who wrote to me after having seen 'Culture in Action' and said that he felt that the project was 'wilfully populist'. I love this phrase – he found it inappropriate because we made it available to everybody.

JK: But I am wondering if part of that kind of criticism involves a notion that because the work so closely addresses issues of social concern, it alludes to a kind of function within the social realm which exceeds its aesthetic grasp. Do you think that some of this criticism occurs because people think the work looks like it is trying to do social work and so people are saying, 'well, how many people did it really help?' If you are going to go down the route of social issues, why leave it at an artistic statement?

MJJ: I think that is part of the criticism, but it is more complex than that. What their argument ignores is that art can work in a manner that is going to touch people in their lives differently than day-to-day social programmes, but reach them and affect them nonetheless. This work was never making claims to functional effectiveness. It was very importantly *art*. So, one asks, if it did not really solve the gang problem, then was it a good use of money? Just because we do not completely solve a social question which a work evokes or even participates in from an aesthetic angle, it is not to say that the gesture and work was not worth doing. Artists are not miracle workers – they are just another alternative. The problem with that viewpoint is that if it is followed all the way through, we could very easily move completely away from having any art at all. And we are all aware that is a direction some are pushing this country in now. But that is not a move that I am in favour of. I think there are certain transcendent things that this work does *because* it is art. I believe, however, that ultimately what the most threatening was the shift in the definition of contemporary art, the potential for there to be a true inclusivity, an embracing of a vast range of people. This is something we talk about making happen in the museum, but do not frequently achieve.

JK: So, when someone comes into a community and says, 'let's make some art together, whether for better or worse', is that part and parcel of what it means to be a public artist? While there is a lot of lip service paid by artists to work within the community, there is also a lot of frustration about it and a feeling that somehow the necessity to work that way damages artists' ability to do what they want and hence makes the work less strong than it might have been. Does a public artist have to say, 'If I'm going to work in the public sphere, I have to prepare myself as an essential part of my practice to let go of that control and give it over to the community'?

MJJ: There is not only one way of doing it. But we do need to move the vocabulary and the ideas forward about art – public art, museum art or whatever. For example, I am advising on the 1996 public art programme for the Three Rivers Arts Festival in Pittsburgh. I did not retain some of the artists because even though they met the criteria, their public art strategies had become formula. They approached the situation knowing what they would do and then wanted to proceed with the least compromise. I prefer working with artists who do not know what they will do at the outset, but come with a purpose, a larger question they want to figure out. That question remains almost to the end, sometimes past the end. With 'Culture in Action' we started with questions and ended up with different questions.

Aspiring sincerely to an international peace based on justice and order, the Japanese people forever renounce war as a sovereign right of the nation and the threat or use of force as a means of settling international disputes. In order to accomplish the aim of the preceding paragraph, land, sea, and air forces, as well as other war potential, will never be maintained. The right of belligerency of the state will not be recognized.

The Constitution of Japan, Article 9.

I wanted to add one other thing, because I am involved in another extensive project which might look like a career anomaly but is not – my work as Consulting Curator to the Fabric Workshop and Museum in Philadelphia. I am working with over 30 artists, continuing the commissioning programme on which the institution was founded, but framing their past activities and pushing to further the direction of working with conceptual artists involved in ambitious projects; some involve object making within the studios, while others happen out in the community, crossing over to this idea of public art that we know. But for all, the projects are developed between the artist, curator and staff, through a collaborative mechanism as a way of moving the art further, moving the thinking further.

This process is based on a partnership of trust that gives freedom to the artist to experiment, fail, try something different. We will use these works as the basis for a travelling exhibition which does not become a single exhibition, my choices and the same choices for each community here and abroad, but is constructed by each venue according to their exhibition history and cultural context. We want to allow for curatorial thinking: What are your programmatic goals? How does this work within your audience and education?

JK: It is interesting to hear the degree to which you really do still speak in the language of the institution. Even with work that appears to be largely extra-institutional, it is still a very important part of your approach.

MJJ: Well, part of the public art's critique of 'Culture in Action' was precisely doing it within the institution, in that case to take the out-of-date model of the host institution, 'Sculpture Chicago', and revise it. They concentrated upon juried exhibitions – the artists were selected based on maquettes and then came together

and worked under a tent for six weeks. They thought they had involved the public and revealed the artistic process. I said 'Process, let me show you process . . . you've got all the words, now let's just actually carry it out, and do it completely differently'.

JK: But when you try to achieve real consensus through a process within the community, are you not then becoming subject to the inherent limitations of that process?

MJJ: I do not think this is as much about consensus as it is about dialogue.

JK: And persuasion?

MJJ: Persuasion only if you are growing and changing, too. If you are going in there just to be persuasive, just to beat people over the head with your idea, then you might as well just make the thing at home and then hope people like it. If you want it to spring organically from the community, it is about dialogue and that grows and changes.

What we were able to do with 'Culture in Action' was to have some people who had lived through the process for weeks or months or over a year, so that by the time it evidenced itself in an object or installation, it was fully embraced and actually a part of them, sufficiently situation-specific to give them a real point of access. I do not think a work of art is about being totally accessible at every moment, at any time, because you and I do not get everything every time we look at it. But it is important that the work of art has something to offer the audience, some handle or some prospect of accessibility so that the audience can begin to deal with it – is it interesting enough to engage them? Does it ultimately have enough of a message or an idea to make their journey worthwhile?

Yukinori Yanagi with The Fabric Workshop, The Forbidden Box, 1995, two panels: iris print on nylon voile, 204 x 116cm each, box: lead and wood, 24 x 36 x 24cm (closed), image: 'Atomic Cloud' (Hiroshima) photo: Asahi Shimbun, Japan. Photo: Will Brown

Cavalier noir, *Auby, 1995. Photo: Jean-Philippe Mattern*

TRUST
GILBERT BOYER
An interview with Bruno Dupont

Comme un poisson dans la ville was an artist-initiated project realised in 1988 and permanently installed on marble plaques and mounted on the sides of a dozen different buildings in Montreal. Gentle poetic phrases provide unexpected urban poetry of everyday history, intimate stories discovered by chance by city dwellers.

The title, *Like a Fish in the City*, is a version of the French expression 'like a fish in water', meaning to be in one's element. Since 1986 Gilbert Boyer has created text-based site-specific installations which explore the paths of public art and urban space. This Montreal-based artist likes the sound of voices, snatches of conversation and his phrases are a tribute to the elements that make up daily life, the here and now. His interventions in the public space succeed in putting us in contact with our private spaces.

How private are public spaces ? This was the question raised by the sixth annual *100 Days of Contemporary Art* organised by Claude Gosselin of the Centre international d'art contemporain in Montreal in 1991. In this event around the theme of public art, Gilbert Boyer recorded the everyday comments of ordinary people, children, friends and lovers, and placed them on circular granite markers along the walking trails of Montreal's Mont Royal Park at the sites where he actually heard them. '*Ah, the sun's coming out. I told you so . . . We'll go the whole way round . . . Not far from here Charles and I had an argument. I can't even remember why any more . . .*' The project entitled *The Mountain of Days* places private conversations in public places and sharpens the interplay between the two realms by the use of granite discs, where instead of solemn statements about historical events or founding fathers, we are confronted with casual voices which might be our own.

I Looked for Sarah Everywhere in the Toronto sculpture garden is a work that speaks directly to the viewer's experience of the city. The work consists of a series of six black granite slabs sunk discreetly into the ground of this public park. On each one a sketchy map and fragments of a handwritten text are carved, detailing the author's search for a fictitious Sarah, a woman he has met in Toronto and wants to see again on this return trip. But Sarah has disappeared and the texts, each one overlaid by a map, plan or sketch, follow the author as he vainly visits Sarah's haunts. Only the central area of each text is reproduced, the missing words at the beginning and end of each line evoking a powerful sense of loss. What emerges is not only the pain of this one missing individual but the isolation of every city dweller.

I Looked for Sarah Everywhere is quietly integrated into its surroundings and offers a counterpoint to the barrage of informational texts and images we encounter daily in our urban environment which invade out innermost thoughts and feelings. In Gilbert Boyer's pursuit of intimacy in a public place, *I Looked for Sarah Everywhere* allows us to construct our own private realities, based on what we do not see.

But for Boyer the ostensible subject matter is secondary to his ongoing exploration of what art is and how it is perceived by the public, the boundaries between art and non-art, frontiers of the perceptible and imperceptible: 'I'm interested in both the public and the art world. But the public thinks of art as something distant. If people like a thing, if it's near to them, they do not think of it as art'. His gallery work is often based on this relationship between the public and contemporary art, the status of the artist in society today (and Gilbert Boyer's place within the museum), notions of art, the art world, the local and international art market. This is demonstrated in a sound installation entitled *Artiste en conversation un jour d'audience* involving three giant door bells in the exhibition 'Pour la suite du monde' at the Musée d'art contemporain in Montreal in 1992 and his 'collection' of galleries: the presentation of floor-plans of well known galleries in major cities throughout the world cut out in vinyl, with information relating to each gallery's professional network in the art world on computer discs exhibited at galerie Michèle Chomette in Paris and galerie Christiane Chassey in Montreal. If art is in the galleries, then collecting the latter means obtaining the art object, its promoter and the double reputation of dealer and artist.

More recently, Gilbert Boyer's proposal for a work to commemorate Montreal's 350th birthday, *Mémoire ardente*, provoked a heated controversy when plans about its installation were announced. Boyer's aim was 'to create an intimate relationship between the public and the commemoration, not something to be seen at a distance, but a work to be experienced personally and individually'. From a distance the sculpture looks like a pink granite cube (almost two metres square) with its rough exterior drilled, at regular intervals, with holes. If one looks through the holes one can see poetic references to Montreal streets and landmark sites, as well as common phrases that have been etched onto the smooth interior surface in both official languages. At its inauguration, the reception to the piece was mixed, to which the artist replied, 'As with people, we have a tendency to judge art by the exterior. But it's also the inside that's important, not only the outside'.

In April 1995, the Lille-based independent association @Art Connexion invited Gilbert Boyer to take up residence in Auby, a small ex-mining town of 8,000 inhabitants in the north of France.

ABOVE: Memoire Ardente (Monument), *Montreal, 1994; BELOW:* I Looked for Sarah Everywhere, *Toronto, 1992;*

The two month residency was set up at the initiative of the town's cultural department with matched funding from the education department of the regional arts council. As this was the first residency of its kind in Auby, @Art Connexion was asked to set up the scheme and liaise with the artist.

The educational aspect of the residence was fundamental and the artist's presence was seen as a way of introducing the community to the notion of contemporary art. The artist-in-residence was invited to set up his own project with the local teachers and school children and there were no expectations on the part of the town hall on the form that this should take. The artist was also asked to realise some sort of presentation of work in the municipal exhibition space which was to serve as an open studio, and contact with local school children and inhabitants was encouraged. Although it was not specified by the town itself, it seemed logical in this particular context to invite an artist with experience and convictions about contemporary art and the public space.

Bruno Dupont, who co-ordinated the project for @Art Connexion, talked to Gilbert Boyer at the end of his residency in Auby.

Bruno Dupont: Why did you accept the invitation to Auby?
Gilbert Boyer: I was interested in the possibility of developing a project in a specific community in which there is practically no contact with contemporary art or the very notion of what contemporary art is, as opposed to painting, sculpture and so on. The fact that the project did not stem from an art institution was already unique for me. Artists are often invited by art institutions to produce a piece of public art for the local population, with the local population. The town of Auby wanted an artist in the town to create some work, to meet people in its schools and outside, and to be available to show how a contemporary artist works and develops a project. The idea of meeting a small community was written into the project from the beginning. Of course, the feasibility of this was much to do with the size of the town and contact with the local inhabitants was actually possible.

I had never been an artist-in-residence before. For the *Urban Paradise* project I was in New York for a period of four months off and on but that experience of working with small groups of people made me want to explore that way of working further, especially since I have always been criticising the lack of contact the general public has with the world of visual arts.

BD: You were not required to produce a permanent commission. What are the advantages of this kind of residency where the final 'product' takes the form of temporary installations?
GB: In the case of permanent works, one of the classic constraints is the question of resistance to time, weather and vandalism which considerably reduces the choice of materials, techniques and methods of installation. What is more, it is often demanded that the works require little or no maintenance. Temporary installations are naturally more flexible and imply a different

approach. They enable experimentation, and explore space and time differently.

A temporary exhibition creates a different vision, another outlook, another approach to reality: the impact is mainly in the mind, on the memory. In a temporary work the artist can explore other sensibilities and the work does not have to deal with the timelessness of the monument as in most permanent work. The work can experience the shorter time concept, it can experience and touch the urgency of a situation.

BD: How did you involve secondary school pupils in the creation and realisation of the work in Auby ?
GB: What was important was that their involvement in the project was optional. Having presented my work, I went back to see them to begin the interviews and started with a list of eight or nine willing students and ended up with 25. The interviews were conducted initially to gather a bank of voice recordings about their understanding of life in the region but, in fact, the exercise turned into a process of trust and confession between the students and myself. They discussed their lives, their families, their hopes and scepticism for what the future held. I was very impressed by their generosity in confiding in me.

Later, I explained what I would like to do with the voices and invited them to work on the installation. The collaboration was set up naturally but it was never imposed and grew from the interest and willingness of the students.

BD: What was the attitude of the teachers you were dealing with?
GB: Firstly, we had to ascertain what the difference was between modern art and contemporary art. In an early discussion I had with some of them, I recall that one of the objections to contemporary art production was that everyday items like garbage or sweets could not be art compared to the beauty of the *Mona Lisa* or a Van Gogh painting. They knew almost nothing about art, they only knew the object known as art, not the art experience or the 'artistic gesture'. They did not know how an artist materialises concepts, visions, feelings or ideas from what is present and contemporary in society. They did not know that such things as blood or cars, for example, can be the oil paint of today. The main reaction of people who have not been in contact with contemporary art is that they have extremely strong prejudices about what art should be. Most of the time their concept of art naturally relates to beauty, hard work and the artist's technical skill, and excludes any other notions. The main exercise was to listen to their concept of art and try to widen those concepts as regards the way an artist works.

One thing I did not want them to forget was to trust their own taste, and develop it. At one point I used the example of wine tasting. You do not know right away if a wine is good or not when you have never really drunk wine because you cannot distinguish the difference. You have to educate your taste first. That does not mean you have to like all great wine. You can still have preferences.

LA PLUIE M A LAISSE UN GRAND MIROIR
D'ASPHALTE. AUJOURD'HUI J AI LE TEMPS.

UN BOUT DE PAPIER TOMBE DU CIEL
SE BALANCE A GAUCHE A DROITE CHUTE
AU RALENTI J AI VOULU LE PRENDRE.

PIQUE DE DEUX GOUTTES NOIRES
UN PAPILLON BLANC SE POSE SUR MA MAIN
SA DERNIERE JOURNEE PEUT-ETRE.

QUELLE CHALEUR!
J EN VIENS PRESQUE A RÊVER DE L HIVER.

JE ME SUIS ARRÊTÉ PRÈS D'ICI
UNE POUSSIÈRE DANS L OEIL.
A LA POINTE DE L ANCIEN HÔTEL DE VILLE
SE TIENT EN ÉQUILIBRE UN OISEAU NOIR.

IL S EVENTE LENTEMENT POUR SE RAFRAICHIR
LES AILES DEPLOYEES.

LEFT: Comme un poisson dans la ville, *Montreal, 1988; RIGHT:* The Mountain of Days, *Montreal, 1991, granite, 8 x 152cm. Photo (above right): André Clément*

Still, when you do not like a wine or a type of wine, you can distinguish why.

BD: Would you agree that you convinced teachers by the explanations you gave but the children needed no convincing about the work?

GB: I do not know if I convinced the teachers. They listened to my rational explanations in the light of previous discussions about what contemporary art was about and most of them tried to use them to look at the work.

In the case of the children, it was quite different. They did not need as many explanations because their concept of what art is was either nonexistent or developing. They were closer to the idea of art simply because it was another experience, because they did not have strong ideas about what it should be. They did not grasp all the aspects of the work but they were open to the confrontation of art. The difference between adults and children is that the adult thinks he or she knows. Children adapt.

One day when I was trying to explain to the students the need to really look at art to experience the work, to discover hidden meanings, I used the image of the extraction of coal to explain the work and the energy we have to spend to find, extract and bring to the surface the source of power and heat, as the meaning of things like art, life, etc.

BD: How did you come to choose the materials you used ?

GB: There was no obligation to use materials from the region but the elements I used were essential to the history and life of the inhabitants of Auby itself, with the presence of the biggest zinc factory in Europe in the town and its mining history. It was obvious that the mining activity had played a great social, economic and political role and that this activity and its demise still affected the lives of the young and old in the region. In the 1980s Auby was also well known for its pirate Radio-Quinquin and the town's fight to maintain an independent opportunity to broadcast other voices – my installation echoed this desire to let other voices be heard by using the voices of the children. When I visited the infant school and saw the children playing with letters on little blocks of wood, I had an idea for an approach to art like the apprenticeship of reading, like inventing a reading scheme.

BD: The title of the piece in the municipal art space was *Cavalier noir* which means 'black horserider' in English but had a specific meaning for the Aubygeois.

GB: Like much of my work in galleries or public spaces, *Cavalier noir* is an installation that implies a physical involvement on the part of the spectator, the literal reading of the work requires an intimate relationship with the work. At Auby I continued to work on the question of communication and the accessibility of art to different publics, and *Cavalier noir* was a sort of metaphor for the reading of an art work. It can also be described as a passage for voices, speech which came from a hole in the floor and went through the window to imply the relationship with the outside space. In mining regions, 'cavaliers' are the elevated tracks on which the wagons transport the coal out of the mines. In this installation, sheets of glass are suspended from the ceiling and the 'cavalier' transport lumps of coal – all stencilled with white letters – piled up along the glass passageway. But the reading of the piled up coal had several meanings. The only word that could be read was seen underneath the glass, the French word *Confiance* (trust, confidence); which is just what the spectator must have, to have trust whilst walking under these fragile sheets of glass, these relationships based on confidence that we try to create with others, that I had tried to establish with the inhabitants of Auby. In the same way, in reading an apparently inaccessible work, one has to look for the essential and bring it to the surface. When I try to explain that trust is the basis for all human relations, whether they be personal, political, diplomatic or economic, I have the impression that I am illustrating a concept. In fact it is the work with the students that showed me the central point of human relations, interventions in the public space, the reading of a work. If there is mistrust, there will be no work in the public space, no communication, no confidence in oneself, no work. Finally, in retrospect, I can see that trust was the whole theme of Auby. Trust began with the students discovering they lacked confidence in themselves and in others; there would be no communication if it was not based on trust, and trusting that it was a work of art, confident that is was full of meaning.

BD: The work you presented in the cellar was haunting. How would you describe it ?

GB: Voices could be heard through the bars of a dark cellar under the exhibition space, as if it were a mining gallery. In the distance there was a little light which barely lit the floor. *Soupirs du Nord* (Northern Sighs) is a selection of little comments, observations, exclamations, questions or desires based on the interviews with the students. On the other hand, *Northern Sighs* is also the listener blocked in front of the gate, confronted with a dark and inaccessible space.

The voices were transferred onto two CDs and seemed to be in dialogue with each other. But the voices were not really speaking to each other, they were talking to themselves in a monologue. These voices speak of solitude, and in their isolation they rest enclosed and the listener is kept outside.

BD: You made another sound piece in an abandoned chapel in the town which made people stop and listen but it also was about the accessibility of art.

GB: In the question of the accessibility of the work there is always the notion of reading, or the apprenticeship of reading a work. In a book by Peter Handke, *A Writer's Afternoon*, I had discovered a text where the writer talks about what a work is. This question is translated into the reading of this extract by primary school children, who are learning to decode letters and words. The reading therefore

Auby, 1995, ABOVE: Voyettes; *BELOW: details of* Cavalier noir. *Photos: Jean-Philippe Mattern*

is not perfect, it either takes on a monotonous tone or there are hesitations. The chapel looks onto the street but the door is locked, and the noises of the passing cars sometimes drown the sound of the reading so one has to listen carefully. When a passer-by on the street listens to the text, the listening/understanding of the work is disturbed.

BD: Another installation in the town was to be found in the 'voyettes'.
GB: The 'voyettes' are little alleyways or short cuts through the bottom of back gardens. They have an intimacy, an unofficial air, and are not marked on the town map. They imply an air of intrusion because they look onto private property and are almost private alleyways, reserved for the initiated. Like *Comme un poisson dans la ville*, plaques of zinc inscribed with words taken from the interviews with the students were inserted into people's gardens behind fences. They are not spectacular, their real incorporation into the urban landscape will come with time as they are integrated into people's daily itinerary and I hope we can arrange for them to be left for at least a year.

BD: How does your 'public work' interact with the work you present in galleries or contemporary art spaces?
GB: For many there seems to be a difference between my gallery work and that found in the public space. For me there is less and less difference and in both cases they are increasingly *in situ*. I develop my exhibitions as if I was developing an intervention in the urban space. I take into account the place, its history, its activity, its public, and in certain cases the role I am playing.

BD: So, do you see yourself as a 'public artist'? And what does 'public artist' mean?
GB: I think the 'public artist' label is not very clear. I would say that the question of public space is linked to the concept of a space for communicating with the public, whether in an urban, advertising, electronic or transport space. The public artist works within these communication networks used by everyone and not only by the 'amateurs' or 'specialists' of the art world.

BD: Is 'public' abstract or concrete?
GB: Public is abstract because it does not define a particular group but all groups. The public becomes concrete when one can identify where they belong, which network. I think there are two worlds, the art world and the rest. And, as artists, we have a tendency to mainly preoccupy ourselves in reaching the art world in the interests of our career to the detriment of other publics. I always bear my public in mind when I prepare a work but that does not mean I do not work to certain criteria of 'quality'. I do not think it is pejorative to take the existence of the public into account.

BD: You are preparing another project with @Art Connexion in Lille, a temporary installation called *Ange interdit* (Forbidden Angel).
GB: Quite by chance I found an abandoned private mansion which seemed like the perfect space needed to create a piece I had in mind with padlocks. *Ange interdit* is a sound installation with a series of padlocks engraved with the words *Ange* and *interdit* enclosed within the courtyard of this mansion. It is an *accessible* and *inaccessible* space, physically closed but visible nevertheless through the bars of the entrance. Passers-by will be presented with this unexpected installation and hear the sound of angels' wings. This will be a poetic space closed on itself but open to the imagination of others. It occurred to me that this was also a sort of metaphor for the reading of a work of art, for the invisibility of art in the world.

BD: Finally, what is the latest news on your controversial *Monument* [*Memoire Ardente*] in Montreal?
GB: Going well from what I have seen and heard. The day I went to the Place Jacques-Cartier there were plenty of people looking inside and walking around to see other sides of the cube. Most of the people I have seen have told me it is working. The new administration, however, is just trying to forget it. The media have done nothing more against it. And the arts magazines are still not talking about public art – as if it was not worth talking about it because it is too low in a hierarchy of genre.

BD: How do the public see the work now?
GB: It is known as 'the cube'. And since it was installed it has become a regular meeting place. But this is not a criteria of success in public art yet.

SPECIFIC EXPERIENCES
SIX BACHELORS, EVEN
Valérie Mavidorakis

In a notorious 1883 lecture, William Morris bluntly observed:

Artists are forced to express themselves, as it were, through a language that the people do not understand. This is not the fault of the artists. If, as some would like to convince them, they tried to come closer to the public and worked in such a way as to respond at any cost to the vague ideas of art held by those who know nothing about it, they would sacrifice their particular gifts and betray the cause of art that they are bound by duty and pride to serve.[1]

Although the problem would not be expressed in such solemn terms today, it continues to exist, and art has yet to find its proper place in the public space. In order to deal with this situation, which is practically a truism, theorists, critics, sociologists and activists of all stripes have developed 'strategies' aimed either at consulting a given social or ethnic group or at associating the population with the conception of the work, scrupulously taking into account the public's expectations and dissecting its supposed reactions so that the art can provide an appropriate response.[2] How to keep the work from getting lost in the twists and turns of the psychology of the masses, who are always ready to sacrifice it on the altar of their sensibilities for alleged political incorrectness? How to present it in a positive way when it is generally perceived as an insult to aesthetics or a misappropriation of public funds? Without all these safety-net strategies, we would practically find ourselves back at Morris's disturbing assertion.

As an alternative to this venerable dilemma, I have come to admire the capacity of some works or projects to shift the debate over public art away from the beaten path. These works seem to me to reflect the genius of certain artists to come up with gestures that escape all normative pressures. I like their openness, their obviousness or their audacity, and I have noticed that they always elicit respect, pleasure or even joy. These works, some of which have not yet been executed, vary considerably in their nature and forms. To begin with, they do not necessarily stem from a public commission although they all involve the public space, ie, the space of opinion and exchange. Nonetheless, they share certain features which allow me to group them together and which at the same time set them apart from the majority of the projects that can be encountered in this context.

First of all, these works share a patent taste for objects from the real world, but they are never pure readymades. These are extraordinary objects or situations, which are familiar, yet slightly out of context. In addition, they are based on the kinds of simple experiences, accessible to everyone, that John Dewey saw as the essence of art: 'In order to understand the meaning of artistic products, we have to forget them for a time, to turn aside from them and have recourse to the ordinary forces and conditions of experience that we do not usually regard as aesthetic'.[3] According to Dewey, objects or events are always a special part or phase of the surrounding world, which leap out at us through their intermediary. Whenever we look at an object we experience a minuscule particle of the world. These works thus offer situations that hover between art and what at first sight does not belong to its sphere. With only a few exceptions, for example, they show little concern for beauty. They may seem beautiful to some, according to their culture, but they can also be judged according to other criteria without losing their interest.

In addition, these experiences are not exactly the ones that today's life gives us the time to have. They slip between all sorts of boundaries that we use to distinguish one kind of experience from another. The fact is that they add to our existence by evoking a gesture, an emotion, a thought or a question more than usual, and they also offer us an extra thought about the world. They place us on a path that we would not necessarily have taken by ourselves. As a result, these experiences can be called 'specific' in the sense that they escape all attempts at categorisation, exactly as Donald Judd's 'specific objects' cannot be understood as either painting or sculpture.

Public art is not generally accepted by 'those who know nothing about art' unless it conforms to their own academic image. But in the case of the works by Lothar Baumgarten, Claudio Parmiggiani, Raoul Marek, Fabrice Hybert, Gérard Collin-Thiébaut and Eric Hattan who I would like to cite, it is not exactly necessary for the public to identify them as works of art in order to appreciate them. This is their strength and their effectiveness. To cite Dewey once again: 'The arts which today have the most vitality for the average person are things he does not take to be art'.[4] These works exist both in and out of the art world, in Arthur Danto's meaning of the word. In, because they do not constitute any break in the production of their creators but rather, are completely consistent with it (indeed, connoisseurs can quickly link these proposals to the pieces they are used to contemplating in museums or galleries). Out, because the neophyte sees them above all as experiences that are attractive, intriguing, amusing, beautiful and so forth, and accepts them as such without knowing, or before knowing, that they are artistic. Through the specific experiences that they provoke, these works thus set off a process of appropriation before they are recognised as art. And their main characteristic is related precisely to this strange phenomenon: something in them makes the public grant them legitimacy without invoking the notion of art. These works thus depend on several non-concentric circles of reception, because they are based on a common property, a collective culture, but, on another level of interpretation, evoke lofty aesthetic references.

Devoid of any didacticism, ideology or demagogy, they do not address a predetermined group in the way that a market survey isolates a target in order to better adapt its tactic for seduction. Rather, they target the public as a whole, allowing all its different elements to find something in them, in a way that is not identical but probably equivalent. This explains how such works can escape traditional distinctions and problems between high and popular art, contemporary art and crafts, art for art's sake and social art, and so forth. Each of the works described below approaches the limits of the notion of art to the point of completely blurring the signs of their recognition.

Lothar Baumgarten and the Bag of Winds in Barcelona

In Barcelona, the destruction of old warehouse areas has opened up the vast Pau Vila plaza that connects the old port to the beachside neighbourhoods of La Barceloneta. This plaza is so long that in spite of the people who come to walk, bicycle or skate there, it seems almost deserted. Numerous benches allow time to pause, but it is above all an open passageway. At night, the red neon of Mario Merz's *Fibonacci* series traces a diagonal line. During the day, it is barely apparent that the ground is punctuated by brown metal in practically the same colour as the surface of the square. It is the difference in the materials that first strikes the eye. At that point, one letter emerges, then others, until, when they are connected, a word pops out of the ground: 'tramuntana', 'mestral', 'ponent' or still others that are less familiar to anyone who is not a Catalan navigator. All the winds, those of the mountains and those of the sea, good ones and evil ones, compete for the space in their elegant letters of steel. And their names, which sometimes glide beyond the square and encroach on the asphalt of the street, make up an archaic litany. Baumgarten has opened up Aeolus's bag of winds, and his work, *La rosa dels vents*, created in 1992, assumes the familiarity of a classic poem.[5] Every word is oriented to the direction of the wind involved, and it is hard to tell whether one feels the breeze before reading its name or vice versa. This space, already endowed with its own aesthetic qualities, now becomes the crossroads of all the winds in Catalonia. Over time, the metal will darken, the trees will grow and the winds, the site and the work will fuse in a subtle sensorial harmony.

This experience can be lived as a kind of nature lesson, or taken in passing, in bits and pieces; it can also suggest a poetic promenade through the associations generated by the words. That may be enough for some. Others may not even pay attention to it; they may not see anything at all. But the connoisseur will recognise with satisfaction the way that Baumgarten has used the language, organised it into lexicons to enclose the sectors of the world that he fills with mental images.

Here, as with the works that follow, the vocabulary used initially operates within a popular culture. All the residents of Barcelona know most of the names enumerated. These words speak to them about an immediate reality in an unexpected way. But what does the Fibonacci series, which has nonetheless become a paragon of public art, have to say to them?

Claudio Parmiggiani's Unexpected Shore

During a stay in Brittany in 1992, Claudio Parmiggiani found himself caught up in contemplating the tides that alternately overflow and outline the remote, uninhabited inlet of Gwin Zegall on the Côte d'Armor. When the water rises, only a few rocks emerge; when it recedes, they are surrounded by a strip of sand and pebbles. The high-tide level leaves its mark on this particularly virgin landscape, devoid of any trace of human presence, by a line of black algae which give concrete form to the idea of perpetual motion. The artist thought of placing a group of oval-shaped black granite stones on this strip, so that the ebb tide would gradually reveal them, and the sea water and light would make them shine like mysterious jewels. The natural rhythm of the elements would thus determine the visibility of the work, which, polished by the undertow, would probably wind up one day as pebbles among the pebbles, and ultimately grains of sand.[6] These enormous, dark eggs could have been deposited by some sea monster risen from the depths. They could open up to give life to fantastic creatures. They represent an unknown emerging from the ocean, an alien. They are perhaps signs of another world, a topsy-turvy world of mysterious origins, peopled by giant beings. The beauty of a landscape evoking a romantic culture is imprinted with the signs of an imaginary macrocosm, as if the proportions of nature suddenly had to be reconsidered.

Parmiggiani has been using the ostrich egg since 1967 for its multiple symbolism of creation and resurrection, magical variations on the scales of the universe, an esoteric and philosophical metaphor. If the sphere, idealised in the sky by the sun, is an absolute but empty form, the egg is the earthly promise of a secret future. The work adds a disturbing strangeness to a site that already houses many legends. The viewer's imagination is stimulated without any indication that an artist's subjectivity is involved. The work is visible, then hidden; its discovery depends on the moment. These few hints of mystery suffice to topple an entire landscape into the uncertainty of perception. Unfortunately, this is only a project proposal, and as yet, a public commission – which is often so quick to evoke responses where there are not always requests – has not been forthcoming. If Baumgarten's *La rosa dels vents* and the work by Raoul Marek that follows basically address the immediate users of their sites and speak to them about their community and their memory, Parmiggiani's project speaks to no one in particular and commemorates nothing other than an unlikely arrival, the promise of a birth.

PAGE 56-59: Lothar Baumgarten, La rosa dels vents, *Barceloneta, Port Vell, Barri de la Ribera, Barcelona, 1992. Photos: (p56 above) Massimo Piersanti and (p56 below) Rafael Escudé*

Claudio Parmiggiani, Untitled, *1992, project for Gwin Zegall, ink and photomontage. Photo: Runquist, Mamco*

The 'Planetary City' According to Raoul Marek

It is 30th June, and a crowd is gathering around the tables that have been set up at the Château d'Oiron for the annual banquet organised for local residents by Raoul Marek. Each person searches for the plate that bears his or her profile and the glass engraved with his or her initials. And on the white napkin, each one will also find the blue imprint of his or her palm. The feast brings together 150 people in what constitutes one phase of the project entitled *La salle du monde* (The Room of the World).[7]

The ordinary visitor who enters this château singularly devoted to contemporary art can admire the dinner service with its anonymous likenesses hung on the wall like the precious pieces of faience that sometimes decorate the dining rooms of family mansions. When not in use, the work, organised in a rigorously egalitarian way, constitutes a fragile portrait gallery awaiting the ritual feast that it convokes every year on the same date. For such a visitor, 'La salle à manger d'Oiron' (The Oiron Dining Room, 1992-93) belongs to the world of art.[8] But for Oiron resident X or Y, it belongs to a collective adventure that is foreign to the codes of the art world.

In order to make the objects for his feast, Marek has in fact recorded the profile, name and hand imprints of Oiron's 150 residents, men, women and children of all ages. The blue line of the faces marks a phase of each person's development in time: the children grow up, the features age, each year several plates remain on the wall because their owners have died. The ritual should thus continue until the death of the last guest.

The artist has reversed the roles that traditionally marked the social hierarchy. In the past, the village was responsible for serving the château, and when feasts were held there, they were involved only as minor actors. Today they are the honoured guests. These plates bear their images like the coins that used to be struck with those of rulers. As a result, they grant each person a privilege that no longer exists but which remains highly symbolic: the access to power.

This is only one part of the vast programme of *La salle du monde*, which, including six public sites in six cities of the world, will address cultural specificities related to the meal as an essential form of being together. Asked about the definition of this 'planetary city', the artist replies: 'I don't know. Others will have to answer this question. Sort of a border project which creates links between the systems. That's what I work with, and through these forms of linking, I offer an extended form of perception for discussion. Inside and outside the art definition'.[9]

For Art-Lovers and Other Curious People: Collecting Gérard Collin-Thiébaut's *Images*

Madame X lives in Strasbourg. Every morning she stamps her ticket for the tram. But over the past few months, this automatic gesture has lost its banality. Madame X's ticket stays in her pocket all day and is then added to the others which have been carefully set aside until she procures the album for arranging them, with all the appropriate captions. Previously, the first thing she did on leaving the tram was to throw the used ticket away. But one day she noticed that there was a nice image on the back, and that intrigued her. A week later, the tickets, placed end to end, already reconstituted a street in Strasbourg, with one facade after the other, not to mention the images of people in old costumes and

those of the city's mayors, whose identity had never preoccupied her before. Madame X first thought that the city had come up with a really original idea. Then she learned that in fact it was an artist named Gérard Collin-Thiébaut who was responsible for the whole concept.[10] While she may not be convinced that her ticket collection is a work of art, as some would have it, Madame X nonetheless considers herself a collector these days.

The modest media selected by Collin-Thiébaut for most of his public interventions serve, in fact, to alter their fates. Tickets for public transportation, parking meters or parking garages, otherwise destined for the trashcan, wind up being appropriated, preserved, elevated for some to the rank of singular objects; for others, to that of art objects.[11] Despite the differences in their motivations, long-term and last-minute collectors alike find themselves propelled by the same desire, Collin-Thiébaut's *Images* bring together different elements of a common heritage, from the most trivial to the most sophisticated (eg, Alsace's renowned soccer players on the one hand, the miniatures of the abbess Herrade of Landsberg's Hortus Deliciarum on the other).

If curiosity is the first step towards knowledge, these images acquire a real social function. They awaken aesthetic and historical consciousness as a form of the 'learning through the object' recommended by the Alsacian pastor John Frederick Oberlin, a 17th-century humanist theologian. This great pedagogue had devoted his prestigious collections to the aim of mastering the world through education in the same way in which the playful little treasures of Collin-Thiébaut function in all humility – except for the fact that the artist now puts himself in the place of the scientist and his images have worth not only because of their knowledge content but also because of their artistic value, based on their status as 'recycled' objects.

Fabrice Hybert Plays the Candy Game

Collecting used objects in one case, using collectors' objects in another: the works of Collin-Thiébaut and Marek are only fully realised when they enter the profane rituals that they imply. With Fabrice Hybert's project, the work's existence depends on its industrial manufacture. Its use will, in fact, exclude it from the ranks of art and propel it into the status of consumer product.

What could be more insignificant that a piece of candy? This is the first thought that comes to mind with regard to Hybert's *Bonbon très bon* (Dandy Candy). In reality, the *Bonbon très bon* has nothing to do with banal sweets. But rather, a remarkable 'polymorphous perverse' object for young and old, and especially for the old. It is the candy you dream of without daring to say so. The taste first of all. Created from algae – perhaps 'Hybertvert' (Hybertgreen), the name of the 'new colour green' invented by the artist – it will contain a new and duly patented taste enzyme. It will thus be quite dandy, as promised, and two laboratories which specialise in sea flora are presently working to perfect it. However, its purpose is not limited to the satisfaction of gourmandise, for this top-of-the-line candy will have multiple uses. In its final form it will offer the choice of being used orally, as a bath product or as a lubricant. Thus it is not directed at the pleasures of the mouth alone, but at all the body's orifices. In this respect, Hybert's *Bonbon très bon* is not simply a delicacy but also a product for ecological wellbeing and a sexual accessory, indeed, a metaphor for a total sexuality.

In order to ensure the public circulation of this miracle candy, the artist has assumed the role of company head by creating Unlimited Responsibility (UR Inc) for the promotion and distribution of the future product. This is certainly not the only case of such a satirical posture on the part of an artist, but once the candy is marketed in supermarkets, as the project envisages, it will escape its roots in the field of art. The fact is that its adaptation to the ecological and polysexual segments of the market make it a fairly subversive, hybrid prototype.

But how is it still, or already, art? First of all, the *Bonbon très bon* will also be sold in museum shops, a sign of its complementary dual identity. Secondly, if we go back to the Oiron Château, we can locate its prehistory: this is the work entitled *La larve du Programme d'entreprise Bonbon très bon* (The Larva of the Dandy Candy Company Programme), which is to this project what Marcel Duchamp's *Green Box* was to his *Large Glass*.[12] Indeed, it contains in the form of notes, images, drawings, video and definitions, all the elements that may lead to its materialisation.[13] Finally, it should be noted that by the distortions of its normal function, its humour, its forms of existence, this project is completely consistent with the complex, ever-expanding networks of Hybert's work. Its public destination outside the art world has no effect upon these features. This distinguishes it from other projects such as the *We got it!* treat manufactured in Chicago in 1993 by Simon Grennan and Christopher Sperandio with twelve workers from a Nestlé subsidiary. The workers developed the product along with the two 'artistic directors', whose self-proclaimed goal was to 'foreground the line worker and enable him or her to reverse positions with management, if only momentarily in the sacred space of art'.[14]

Eric Hattan's Ghost Telephone

To wrap things up, imagine that you are on the plaza in front of the telephone company building in Biel, Switzerland. Obviously, there are public telephone booths, but suddenly, one of them starts ringing insistently even though no one is inside. Impelled by an irresistible curiosity, you answer it. Surprise: a voice announces the time in Honolulu. You realise there is an eleven-hour time difference between Switzerland and Hawaii. You hope that the voice of the speaking clock will keep counting the seconds so that you can pursue your sudden exotic revery. But the call comes to an end. Something in this phone booth prolongs your astonishment. Since you answered impulsively, you did not notice anything in particular. But you feel something disquieting beyond the strange phenomenon that has just taken place. But of course: everything in this phone booth is oversized, and you are disoriented by it. You have the impression of being reduced to the size of a child, or begin wondering if the world has suddenly undergone a change of scale.

This is Eric Hattan's project, *Zeitreise (Die Ueberquerung der Ozeane)* – Journey in Time (Crossing the Oceans). It is currently being carried out in the context of a one per cent for art at the new telephone company headquarters in Biel. Its functioning is determined by chance: the telephone rings sixteen times in twenty-four hours, day and night, and connects with talking clocks in other cities from sixteen different time zones.[15] The encounter with the work thus depends on the contingencies of the moment. The telephone booth and the phone, meanwhile, are perfectly identical to the usual ones except that they have been enlarged by 20 per cent.

Beneath its false transparency, this work is subtly subversive. The new telephone company building is in fact an expression of the technological power and global efficiency of the telephone medium. Thus the artist is proposing an intervention which uses this omnipotence to its own benefit and places it anecdotally at the disposition of the public. The necessary technical feats defy the abilities of the sponsors, who are trapped by the rigidity of their own norms (it would appear that manufacturing a giant telephone is hardly child's play) and the financial constraints of its networks. Hattan is no stranger to public commissions, and his interventions often do their best to catch the sponsors off guard or drive them into a corner with their contradictions, while the objects or situations he proposes always manifest a curious mixture of enigma and simplicity. They function as political criticism in relation to the government, while offering the public a poetic reality. Once again, Hattan's artist status gives him access to the public space and allows him to produce responses which are both precise and ambivalent but never identified as works of art in their social context.

None of the six cases cited here belongs to the classic categories of public art – painting or sculpture – or even the broader, less conventional categories that have nonetheless been widely developed – architectural art, design art, lighting art, etc. Each one is an original proposition that neither refers to a model nor creates one in turn. These works are all related to a site considered in its physical, symbolic, social, aesthetic or economic dimension but never in a purely formal one. All of them, in their own ways, target the essence of the site: a square buffeted by the winds, wild beach, a village community, supermarkets, public transportation, the headquarters of a public utility. Each of these sites is envisaged according to the kind of behaviour it inspires among its users or the population it attracts. Thus, these works nearly always determine a practice or an activity; but by breaking completely with the functional, they displace gestures into the realm of the spontaneous and the unexpected, into a specific experience that is at once totally familiar and unique.

In addition, their position in relation to the sponsor breaks all conventions. These are either projects defined prior to any official commitment (Parmiggiani, Hybert) or responses that defy official expectations (Baumgarten, Collin-Thiébaut, Marek, Hattan). Since these propositions integrate the social parameters of their sites, the symbolic profit they generate can always be lived as a specific experience in itself, without being represented as an artistic event. Hence, when they encounter rejection, it comes not from the public but from those who have commissioned it.

*Raoul Marek, La salle du monde,
Château d'Oiron, 'La salle à
manger d'Oiron', 1992-93*

ABOVE: Fabrice Hybert, La larve du Programme d'enterprise Bonbon très bon, *Château d'Oiron, 1993;* BELOW: Raoul Marek, Permanent display of plates, *La salle à manger d'Oiron*

The artists I have cited have managed to displace the problems generally tied to public art, and have done so without betraying themselves or denying the difficulties of this arena, by taking into account their obligation of readability and exchange. 'Scribbling on a monumental scale brings into play forces of integration that raise the artist above his little ego', suggests Edgar Wind with irony.[16] In these works, the artist's identity retreats behind the experiences called into play. And the legitimacy acquired by their creator in the field of art is in no way the sole justification of their place in the city, as is so often the case. Who cares, basically, where these works come from and who decided on their existence? They do not impose themselves by force; they slip naturally into the consciousness. Nothing in them expresses the exasperating self-satisfaction of the work that cries out: 'Look at me, I'm part of art'. On the contrary, everything about them corroborates John Dewey's assertion that, 'Where egotism is not made the measure of reality and value, we are citizens of reality and value, we are citizens of this vast world beyond ourselves, and any intense realisation of its presence with and in us brings a particularly satisfying sense of unity in itself and with ourselves'.[17]

Translated from the French by Miriam Rosen

Notes

1 William Morris, text of lecture at University College, Oxford, November 14, 1883, first published in *To-day*, Feb-March 1884; also 'Art in a Plutocracy', *Against Elite Art*.

2 See, for example, *Art in Public*, edited by Susan Jones; *Mapping the Terrain: New Genres in Public Art*, edited by Susan Lacy, Bay Press, Seattle, 1995; *Critical Issues in Public Art*, edited by Harriet F Senie and Sally Webster, Harper/Collins, New York, 1992.

3 John Dewey, *Art as Experience* (1934), Wideview/Perigee Books, New York, 1980, p4.

4 *ibid*, p5.

5 This work is part of a group of commissions for the 1992 Olympics (also including Mario Merz, Rebecca Horn, Jannis Kounellis, J Muñoz, Jaume Plensa, Ulrich Rückreim, James Turrell). See Gloria Moure, *Urban Configuration*, Ediciones Poligrafa and Olimpiade Cultural, Barcelona, 1994, which documents this project.

6 See the drawings for this project (which actually dates back to 1970 with the idea of filling a gallery with 50cm of dirt topped with eggs) in the catalogues *Claudio Parmiggiani, Zeichnungen*, Mathildenhöhe, Darmstadt, 1992-93, p84, and *Parmiggiani, Disegni*, Palazzo Publico-Museo Civico, Siena, 1995, p67.

7 See Raoul Marek, *La salle du monde*, exhibition catalogue, 2 vols and video cassette, Akademie Schloss Solitude and Aachen, Neueraachener Kunstverein, Stuttgart, 1994-95; Kunsthalle, Berne, 1995.

8 *La salle à manger d'Oiron* was made possible by a public commission from the Délégation aux Arts Plastiques of the French Ministry of Culture.

9 *op cit*, Marek, p26.

10 Gérard Collin-Thiébaut's *Images* (1994-) for the Strasbourg tram are made possible by a public commission from the Communauté urbaine de Strasbourg and the Délégation aux Arts Plastiques of the French Ministry of Culture. The project is intended to last for five to ten years. Three other artists were also commissioned to create works for the new tram line: Barbara Kruger, Jonathan Borofsky and Mario Merz (with another Fibonacci series), along with the poets of the Oulipo group. See Catherine Grout, *Le tramway de Strasbourg*, Editions du Regard, Paris, 1995. (See pXII of this issue).

11 These works include tickets for the Grenoble tram (January 1994), for parking meters in Lyons (1991) and for the Lyon Park Auto garage in Lyons (1993-96).

12 *La larve* is a current commission from the Délégation aux Arts Plastiques of the French Ministry of Culture for the Chateau d'Oiron.

13 For a detailed description of *La larve*, see Cristelle Alin and Blanche Tanwery, 'Bonbon très bon', *Laboratoire pour une expérience du corps*, Presses Universitaires de Rennes, Rennes, 1995, pp62-67.

14 See Mary Jane Jacob, 'Eight Projects', *Culture in Action (Sculpture Chicago)* Bay Press, Seattle, 1995, pp114-121.

15 In addition to Honolulu, other cities include Sydney, Tokyo, Peking, Bangkok, New Delhi, Karachi, Tehran, Moscow, Johannesburg, Paris, London, Rio de Janeiro, New York, Mexico City, and Vancouver.

16 Edgar Wind, *Art and Anarchy*, London, 1969.

17 *op cit*, Dewey, p195.

FIN DE STATIONNEMENT AUTORISE
DATE   HEURE
261 10:58 LY
18/09/91   05,00 ORANGE
PRIX

055974   Le Perugin - l'Ascension du Christ, (détail).
                1496-98 - Musée des Beaux-Arts - Lyon
LYON PARC AUTO - LYON FIGARO - GÉRARD COLLIN-THIÉBAUT - ART/ENTREPRISE

TICK'ART

Gérard Collin-Thiébaut

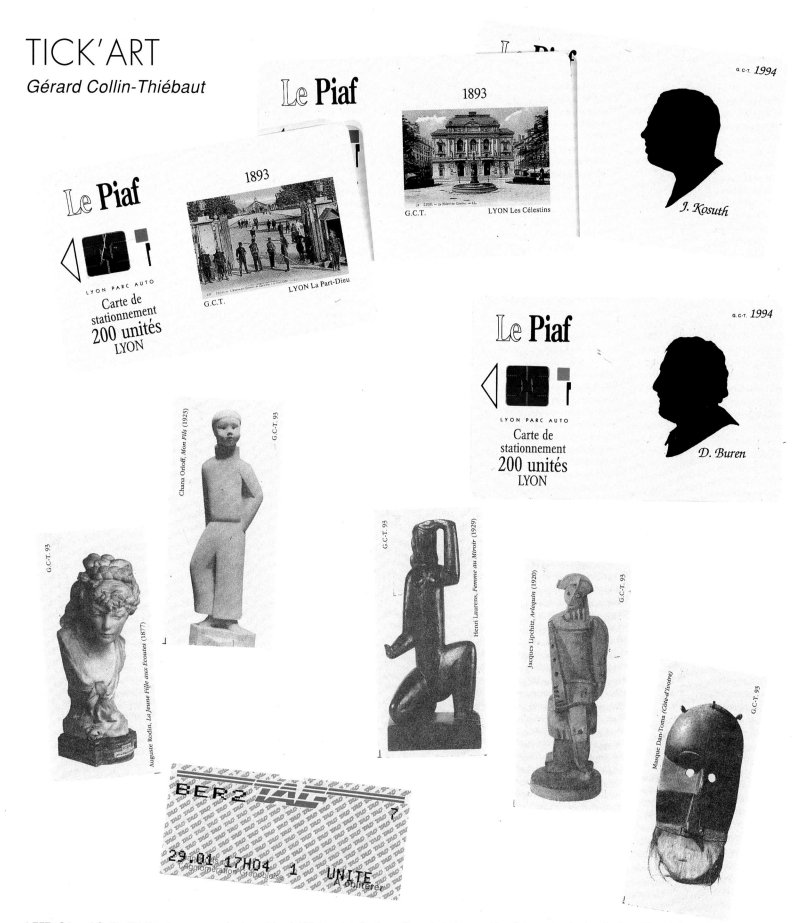

LEFT: *Gérard Collin-Thiébaut was commissioned by Art/Enterprise for Lyon Parc Auto to provide pictures for the back of parking tickets distributed across 90 parking meters in the city centre. Twelve pictures were needed to reconstruct an important chosen painting from the city's Musée des Beaux-Arts – Perugino's* Ascension of Christ. *The other two pictures – close-ups of what are presumed to be disguised self-portraits of the Italian artists in the painting – were intended to be kept separately, perhaps in a pocket, a wallet or a handbag. Each parking meter distributed four different pictures. Anyone wanting to collect the entire set had to find the other meters. These were easily recognisable, as each had stickers with the following printed message: 'Lyon Parc Auto has the pleasure of presenting you with a picture by the artist Gérard Collin-Thiébaut. The date and hour printed on your parking ticket make this an original work. By acquiring twelve pictures you will be able to piece together Perugino's* Ascension of Christ*'.*

The following essays by Mark Lewis and Johanne Lamoureux were taken from the book which followed the exhibition 'Queues, Rendezvous, Riots: Questioning the Public in Art and Architecture'.

The exhibition 'Queues, Rendezvous and Riots' was presented at the Walter Phillips Gallery at the Banff Centre for the Arts in Canada in 1992, both in the gallery and also in other locations on the campus. Works by Vera Frenkel, Elizabeth Diller and Ricardo Scofidio, and Rodolfo Machado and Jorge Silvetti were installed in the Walter Phillips Gallery; Marik Boudreau with Martha Fleming and Lyne Lapointe, and Jeff Wall and Dan Graham proposed works that were exhibited both in the gallery and in satellite locations; while Dennis Adams made a proposal for a permanent installation in the building next to the proposed site.

The anthology, edited by the Toronto-based architect, George Baird, and Vancouver-based artist, Mark Lewis, explores the social and cultural ideas shaping today's public spaces and how artworks and buildings function when they embrace notions of 'the public' which no longer prevail.

PUBLIC INTEREST
MARK LEWIS

The *public* art of our cities. Is it simply a token investment (in every sense of the word) in the city's architectural organisation? Or is it an acknowledgement of the aesthetic experience necessary to make citizenship meaningful? And if so, what are the models, utopian or otherwise, that a modern city might set its sights on emulating? Can we imagine a place where, or time when, the occupation of the city and a certain aesthetic experience were commensurate?

The citizens of ancient Greece, the citizens of Rome, and more recently the citizens of Paris, and even of New York, experienced the city in many ways as a place to be enjoyed. We are familiar with the limits of this experience, indeed the limits of citizenry; we know that even to talk of the aesthetic experience of these places and these times is at once to acknowledge the barbarism upon which they were built. But nevertheless it would be foolish to deny that for those who could enjoy it, the construction of the city – of the public realm – was studied in part with a mind to what we could call the aesthetic rights of those privileged few. Citizenship today is more universal, and we might have reason to expect, then, that the aesthetic experience of the city, previously reserved for the privileged few, would be a central part of this new extended franchise. Posed simply, we could ask if our cities today are organised with aesthetic rights in mind? Or, to ask the question a little more rhetorically, is there any continuity between Athens, Rome, Paris and New York, on the one hand, and the city that increasingly most of us are forced, by reason of work or love, to reside in – the city of the shopping mall and the extended suburb, the city of Toronto, Edmonton, Vancouver, Minneapolis, Houston and Columbus, Ohio? Indeed, should there be?

We hear a great deal today about the importance of public art. An abundance of exhibitions, conferences, books and essays testify to the fact that it has become the *lingua franca* of curators, museum administrators and all those who are concerned to enlarge art's franchise. Public art has increasingly also become a small but integral part of the plans for large scale developments in our cities, and in this respect developers have responded to pressure brought to bear by administrators, government officials, and even artists. This imperative to build and create public art presupposes that there are indeed places that are meaningfully public; that today's city is, in other words, capable of delivering a certain public experience. We need to be certain that this is the case (or certain of the degree to which it is not the case) before we simply deliver to the city objects and markings whose meanings depend greatly on the framing effect of their occupation, public or otherwise.

Increasingly we learn that the possibility of aesthetic involvement in the city is seriously atrophied and, if it exists at all, it is only in the most tangential and inconsequential forms – forms that de Certeau and the Situationists felt obliged to identify as the aesthetic practices of everyday life. We might feel entitled to ask if the crossing of a road against the red light or returning home in a way not detailed according to economics and ergonomics really counts as a significant aesthetic experience.

It would probably not be too difficult to argue, then, that in its most general formulation what is being proposed with public art projects and programmes is less an aesthetic *of*, and more an aesthetic *for*, the public realm – a sort of last minute addition that unwittingly acknowledges the increasing failure of the so-called public realm to entertain the possibility of an aesthetic experience. If this is the case, the rhetoric of art's public involvement might run the risk of passively colluding with this denuding of public life, for in extinguishing their responsibility of protecting absolutely that utopian experience of public life (a responsibility that we might suggest has been the provenance of the enlightenment museum) our 'cultural guardians' might end up introducing the diminished possibilities of *today's* public life into the museum. Would the space between Disney and aesthetic rights even be worth measuring?

Central to the experience of the work of art is the dialectical relationship between form and content. Historically, the relationship between these two has been experienced as an impossible reconciliation (this would be art's difference, so to speak). Expressions like 'form follows content' and 'no content without form' are correct only to the extent that they recognise the difference with which aesthetic judgement must proceed. They are incorrect insofar as they might judge that that difference will be reconciled to the benefit of one term or the other. The commission of a work of art for public display, the desire for such a work, is often predicated on just such a reconciliation of art's dialectic, for this imaginary work must commit itself in advance to exigencies that have the effect of radically diminishing the aesthetic dimension of its experience. For instance, most public works are required to engage with specific interests (community or corporate, for example), interests that are defined before the interrogation of what art in the public sphere might be, an interrogation that, according to the inner laws of art cannot precede its formal experimentation. To talk of interest here is not simply to acknowledge the whole slew of laws and edicts that in turn forbid and allow certain expressions and images in the 'public realm'. These restrictions are simply a matter of an absolute content and art today really has no commitment in this direction.

We need to be clear here, or we risk chasing the tail of a fast disappearing but nevertheless reassuring lure: censorship in art does not exist. Of course it exists in atavistic forms, but today in the West there is nothing that cannot be said, nothing, that is, that when released (as everything eventually is) can in any way mitigate an assumption of liberation, revolution or victory. And this is not simply to affirm the pithy truism that art is no longer *the shock of the new*. Rather it is to underline the fact that the intimate bond that once tied interdiction to art's *modus operandi* (its historical and delicate attempts always to circumvent the laws and protocols that forbade its invasion into certain territorial subject matters of the state, the church or the privileged) has long since expired. Art is free to represent what it likes with regard to subject matter. This is its obligation, an obligation that will not be extinguished simply by local legislation or even by imprisonment. To talk of art being banished or censored, or at least to speak of that as art's primary engagement, is strictly speaking, wrong. To argue otherwise is perhaps reassuring (if your stake is in interdiction and in trying to recreate the possibility of *shock*) but it is a conceit of increasingly obvious proportions.

No, the interest that we might find to have so undermined the possibility of a truly public art, or at least undermined the possibility of properly investigating its definition as such, is one that has, in advance of any real production, been imposed upon this art – a functional *a priori*. In other words, public art must have a function and its total operation must be on behalf of that functionalism, a mimetic relation that will guarantee that this art of the public domain will never simply be itself. With regard to this functional *a priori*, there seem to be at least two common sense imperatives which guarantee that the former remains the putative content of so much of the public art that institutions and officials have championed, indeed allowed.

The first imperative is that this art, a public art outside the museum, must function differently. Why? Because it must answer to the expectations of those for whom the experience of the work of art is an alien concern (they do not, for instance, visit museums regularly). But then do we not run the risk of simply reaffirming that very alienation, assenting to the division of labour that allows some to engage (and others not to engage) with art's essential propositions? At the very least it underlines the difference between the museum and its other, indeed designating an 'out there'; the public realm as *being* the other of the museum. This imperative not only demands that *alienation* be taken into account (and presumably overcome), but because it establishes alienation as a central preoccupation of the work of art, it also insists that the work (or the process of its production) attend to what is often called 'accountability'. To wit: this art outside the museum, but in the place that local people have their history, must respond to that history and recognise the place where it is made. Why? Because the people who live and inhabit that space have the

right to determine what its organisation, aesthetic or otherwise, should be. While it would be difficult to argue, *inter alia*, against that right (indeed the idea of an aesthetic right to the city would seem to include just this sort of franchise), we might want to know how these rights are to be adjudicated and represented. Further, what kind of occupation would determine if one person's stake in that adjudication was more immediate, more pressing than anyone elses? It is worth remembering that accountability, historically mandated by the state through and by its various national and local interests, gave us the commemorative monument. Today, with accountability still the test of much public art, we risk being the grateful recipients of even more monuments, 'democratic' monuments perhaps, but monuments all the same.

As soon as any one or any group begins to speak on behalf of a given community, what is revealed (often because of the need to keep it repressed) is an acknowledgement of the contamination of public rights by private interest. This is not to suggest that private interest is alien to the aesthetic experience of the public sphere; on the contrary, it is to acknowledge the dialectic of public and private that makes the experience of the public realm so significant, so radically public. Think here of the many historical public figures, including the much maligned *flâneur*, who have peopled the public realm and indeed brought it to 'life'. For these figures to enjoy the public realm, it was necessary to both feel the ineluctable draw of anonymity, to become lost in the crowd, so to speak, while at the same time experience the public, or the crowd as spectacle, as cinematic frieze seemingly organised for their or *your* private contemplation. While we might be able to describe this contamination of public and private, this precarious sense of 'publicness', we certainly cannot design it. This is the Achilles heel of the modern, or perhaps we should say, hypermodern city: it needs to plan, to design, to have everything in place before it dares to call itself a city (and the mega development projects are just one sign of this desire for an urban *gesamtkunstwerk*). At the risk of introducing yet another problematic history, we could say that the hypermodern city – the city of Vancouver, especially with its development of the former Expo lands, is exemplary here – would like to stage-manage montage, or at least assemble in a totalised form what heretofore had been brought together without the conceit of a total vision. It is nothing radical to insist upon montage, or at least the montage of public and private as what has provided the modern city with many of its public possibilities. It is important, then, to acknowledge the fundamental relevance of the dialectic of public and private in what, strictly speaking, it is now difficult to call the public realm. Moreover, if we resist the temptation to believe that these conflicting interests can or even should be reconciled, it will bring us one step closer to releasing public art from its own obligatory interest.

The second imperative is that this art, outside the museum, but inside a place where people come to work, rest and play, must practically serve these forms of occupation. Chairs, tables, signs and drinking fountains are only the most obvious exemplifications of this art that has a functional form, though architectural decoration and other public markings could just as easily be imagined.

These two imperatives, then, often burden the public work of art with the obligation to deliver formal solutions to a content already defined, and these solutions can be caricatured as having two very general models: the commemorative monument and the architectural or functional form. Insofar as these are the expectations for a public work of art, they are also its historical antecedents and the extreme limits against which it must at least expect to be read and judged. There are a number of ways in which these obligations can be resisted. Perhaps the least obvious, but certainly not the least interesting, might be to embrace these obligations without pretence, and to embrace them less as contents to be refracted formally, but rather as formal propositions to be transformed dialectically. With obligatory contents (accountability, public alienation, functional models) rhetorically restaged as formal propositions, the irreconcilable dialectic of the work of art within the public domain may be allowed to re-emerge as a problem. It may be that the public realm does not exist; it may be, in other words, that the complicated and dialectical relationship between public and private, necessary for an experience of the public sphere, is disavowed or even impossible in today's cities. But this should be no reason for art, when sited in this non-public place, to give up on its responsibility to refuse those very interests that would guarantee the disappearance of the dialectical relationship that is essential to both art and, for the want of a better word, publicness. Two examples of an engagement with the dialectic of art and its publicness can be found in the following.

The Pyramid and the Wedge: The Monument and Its Waste

In 1918 the Russian architect Nikolai Kolli made a proposal for Lenin's *Monumental Propaganda*, a proposal that was eventually erected in plaster form for the May Day celebrations of the same year. In some respects *The Red Wedge Cleaving the White Masses* is a three-dimensional articulation of the familiar revolutionary emblem that was used to depict the Bolshevik's fight against the invading 'White Armies'. It is also, however, a remarkable critique of the project of monumentality. In Kolli's work the red wedge literally splits open the plinth that supports it, thus presenting the internal and irreconcilable contradiction lying at the heart of a project intending to commemorate, with monuments, the achievements of the revolution. On the occasion of the May Day celebrations to honour the demise of the Ancien Régime and the continuing victory of the revolution, Kolli's monument exacts a critique of monumentality but only at the price of its own failure to escape the very conditions of monumentality.

Revolutions, by definition, cannot be static and eternal: in order to continue their claims to be revolutionary, they must be (permanently) against permanence. Revolutions, however, must also address the question of their own practical hold on power: if a revolution is 'victorious' it will by necessity seek to represent its 'victory', so that it may be historicised, legitimated and guaranteed.

Kolli's wedge can be read, then, as an emblem of this very contradiction: it keeps alive the dialectic of permanence/impermanence, not just as a problem of monumentality but as a problem for the representation of the revolution itself. A similar acknowledgement of this dialectic is to be found in the 'Theory of Ruins' formulated by Albert Speer with the expressed support of Hitler himself. In this case it was a question of presenting the Nazi Reich as a ruin, precisely to achieve the effect of historical permanence; to acknowledge the demise of the regime in a way that suggested that it would be remembered as the antiquity of the future. If Kolli's monument marks the death of the monument, it does so by insisting that the problem of monumentality continues, not necessarily in its proper place – as the physical manifestations of a regime's occupation of the public realm – but elsewhere in the internal contradiction that will dominate the revolution which, when resolved, will inevitably bring about its very demise. As the revolution approaches the condition of monumentality, its 'guardians' will quickly become the new Ancien Régime. In this respect, as much as Kolli's monument is a tomb for monumentality, it is also a tomb for the revolution. As Derrida has shown, the tomb commemorates the disappearance of something (life) by attesting to its perseverance:

This double function belongs to the funerary monument. The body of the sign thus becomes the monument in which the soul will be enclosed, preserved, maintained, kept in maintenance, present, signified. At the heart of this monument the soul keeps itself alive, but it needs the monument only to the extent that it is exposed – to death – in its living relation to its own body. It was indeed necessary for death to be at work – the Phenomenology of the Spirit describes the work of death – for a monument to come to retain and protect the life of the soul by signifying it.

Jacques Derrida, *Margins of Philosophy*.

Another project, although at first sight might not seem to qualify as public art at all, nevertheless continues, albeit unwittingly, Kolli's grave reflections. On April 13, 1989, *The New York Times* announced that Staten Island planned to construct out of New York's garbage a unique monument that would dominate the familiar New York skyline. Somewhat improbably, the Staten Island authorities were preparing to build a giant, thirty-million-ton pyramid that, when completed (anticipated in 2005), would have been as high as the Statue of Liberty. *The New York Times* article kindly included alongside the illustration of the planned pyramid of garbage, an image of the Great Pyramid of Giza, showing how the Staten Island authorities would manage to double in size and volume the historical antecedent. The scheme was utilitarian (the city has to dispose of its garbage somehow) but it was also designed with a monument in mind: to remind New Yorkers of how important garbage is. Waste in this example is produced as a monument to the city's trace of its own occupations, of the occupations of those who inhabit its publicly defined, civically defended and legally inscribed borders. Rapidly disposed of (more rapidly in some areas than in others) garbage must nevertheless reappear somewhere else as the reminder of its temporary disappearance from the place where it was first deposited and accumulated. It does not matter how far you remove it from its source, it will always return in one form or another. Perhaps the most common form of that return is in the environmental damage that it has come to represent. Or in the case of developing countries, its return is in the images of the poor whose scavengings through the mountains of waste testify to the continuing and residual exchange value of garbage (here the 'garbage scavengers' literally take the waste back into circulation, back into the city to be sold). What in any case has become increasingly clear is that while garbage can indeed be disposed of and removed to another place, from this other place it will immediately and ceaselessly plot its return (in the form of acid rain, ozone, contamination) and demand to be treated and removed again and again.

The Egyptians built *the* pyramids and New York would like to build *pyramids of garbage*. Perhaps there is some continuity between the experience of the city of old and our own putative public occupations. But this would only be a highly qualified commensuration of experience. What is strikingly commensurate, however, is the formal and ideological connection that the pyramid of garbage shares with Kolli's wedge. The dialectical relationship between the city and its garbage or more properly, the dialectical tension that would divide the city against its own public definition (the waste is the evidence of a certain public occupation) resonates with Kolli's attempt to bring base and monument together even as he splits the one with the other. The garbage pyramid reintroduces as monument what cannot be allowed in the city. The compulsion of the public sphere to attempt foolishly to (temporarily) evacuate itself of the very signs of its corporeal inhabitations (an irony that is the unmistakable target of the pyramid of shit), is a 'futile' and impossible gesture – one that Kolli's monument presciently identified as existing between the revolution and its desire for monumental commemoration. Both monuments – Kolli's and the one that would properly belong to the waste of New York – are tombs (in the Derridian sense of reversal), therefore testifying to the continued perseverance, even in decomposition, of problems of permanence and monumentality, of impermanence and commemoration, and of waste in the place of its expunction. If these problems are no longer really on site, if they remain veiled and scarcely recognisable, they are nevertheless always contiguous and dialectically implicated in every public project that might wittingly or unwittingly have an aesthetic engagement with the public realm.

The pyramid of garbage is, of course, Kolli's wedge in reverse.

Instead of splitting its base open, the excrescence of the earth, or rather the excrescence that is the industrial and domestic metamorphosis of the earth's contents, spits upwards, destroying the useful landscaping of the cityscape. Shit and garbage protrude from the base that can contain them no longer and in so doing this pyramid of garbage revisits the history of modern sculpture. Rodin, then Brancusi and finally Robert Morris spelt the end of the regime of the sculptural object separated from the world by the effect of its base. Their work may have marked the end of a regime that would have the object, separate, venerated and stable but as *any end* will eagerly announce, the base will return, periodically and veiled to varying degrees. It will return as the excrescence of the sculptural object, of the statue in particular, but of everything that will attempt in the public sphere to mark, structure and commemorate certain types of occupation, bodies or imaginary events. Between Rodin and Morris, then, Kolli's wedge reprises the privilege of the base, resurrects it without nostalgia, simply as the reminder of the ghost that, even as Morris installs his mirrored cubes in Castelli's own white cube, will continue to haunt any sculptural project.

The pyramid of garbage recycles Kolli at the same time as it tips its hat to Piero Manzoni. It begs the question whether we can ever resolve the contradiction between a public space that requires rigorous order and cleansing with the inhabitations that quite naturally spoil all such attempts at expurgation. In juxtaposition with Kolli's impossible monument to the revolution, the pyramid might also suggest that, with the aesthetic forms that from time to time will be introduced into the public realm as something extra, we might, when imagining a public art, be usefully drawn in the old direction of monumentality – not because monuments gracefully perform aesthetic acts of public beauty, but rather because, as the discussion above on *interest* suggested, it is in the monument that we can find a history of public art and also *the* history of all those who would have us remember their particular form of political organisation, their form of the organisation of the public sphere, even if it was only in theory. If Alois Reigel was clear that such a commemorative project, such a remembering, is impossible, then this does not at all contradict the fact that the public, whoever he or she is, still longs for such a job of monumentality. We could say, following Bataille, that the monument (with its base) is the job of all public art, the ineluctable pull of its heretofore unexorcisable able demons. Abstraction, then, as the sign of the removal of the monument and its plinth from the public sphere, is perhaps like the pyramid of garbage – a reminder that the base of everything has slid a little deeper. However, in its rank decrepitude, it persists.

QUESTIONING THE PUBLIC
JOHANNE LAMOUREUX

What *Queues, Rendezvous and Riots* questioned was the very possibility of the *public as a notion*, not as a person, a group of persons, or a group of group of persons.

Viewed as such, the exhibition can be read as an elaborate construct that plays with two main traditions of public intervention symptomatic of the crisis within modernity: the monument and agitprop. The first was taken up primarily by the type of artworks that had been selected (and one could sense there the determining presence of George Baird, *architect*): as a body of works, the exhibition was indeed concerned with the possible reformulation of the monumental, its rescaling, reorientation, refunctionalisation. The exhibition stood as a statement on the public signifier.

Yet, I would argue, the selection and presentation of these works was only part of the curatorial activity involved. *Queues, Rendezvous, Riots: Questioning the Public* had an unusual curatorial paratext, not in the form of a catalogue or labels, but in the agitprop photomontage that greeted the visitor at the entrance of the exhibition and that indexed the first part of the exhibition's title: *Queues, Rendezvous, Riots*. In the same vein, the curators undertook to place on the grounds of the campus anonymous signs – shields of plastic orange fencing – next to the pieces of sculpture acquired over time by the Centre. The works are permanently displayed on site in such a mode of invisibility that no one could even make sense of the bright orange indexes calling attention to them. (Here, one is reminded of Lewis's own practice as an artist. These curatorial interventions reflect on the somehow necessary ephemerality of contemporary public interventions today.) This intervention seemed to denounce the conditions of insignificance and indifference whereby public markers can occupy a site and remain there only if they are both visible and inconsequential.

The curatorial decision to take action *around* the exhibition reveals the other *versant* of the project. Queues, rendezvous and riots are all modalities of action and appearance in public; they are modes of *public affect*, understood here as the permeability of space and subject in the realm of affect: the passivity of waiting (queues), the celebration of intimate, individual encounters (rendezvous), the clashing contestation of space (riots). In a sense, the curatorial paratext invited one to conceive of these figures and modalities of social encounters as contemporary public signifiers that challenged the abstraction of 'questioning the public'. Indeed it did activate a certain tone, a rhetoric resistant to the expected erasure of any editorial statement on the curators' part.

The curatorial gesture of indexation once again focused attention on the public marker itself. It called attention to the message, in the sender-receiver structure of communication, or to what has been called the utterance. Now, if the curators chose, both in the exhibition's paratext and in the selection of artworks, to stress that dimension of public art, they will, at first glance, appear to be promoting a rather modernist statement. I would argue that, in so doing, they went precisely to the heart of the matter and showed how, paradoxically, this is the crucial blind spot in the postmodern debate on the public.

As I attempted to relate the core of the exhibition to its paratext, I found myself constantly shifting the grammatical status of the term *public* from noun to adjective, as if the only problem with the exhibition had been its title, and the only problem with its title was a missing noun that, once found, would reduce the term public to some descriptive ornament and clarify the terms of the discussion. For some time, cultural discourses have urgently discussed and disputed the formulation of the public[1] in the singular form, as an unsizeable, ever-elusive yet all-inclusive, monolithic entity.

In the critique of the singular form of *the* public, two *grammatical* strategies operate. The first maintains the public as a noun, either as a notion in ruin or as a kaleidoscopic all-encompassing term. It contests the global reference of public by adding an *s* and producing a virtually infinite multiplication of fragmented publics whose enumeration brings to mind a Borgesian list. The resulting figure of fragmented publics – many different groups of receivers – in the field of art practices, echoes a situation that we are familiar with in other aspects of society: the representation of the *social* as a mosaic of minorities and the demise of a (fantasised) consensus it has entailed; the parliamentary activism of specialised lobbyists at the political level; and on the communication level (with all its economic determinations), the targeting of more narrowly defined groups of consumers by the new marketing strategies and the rhetoric of publicity. These diverse manifestations of fragmentation should not blind us to the fact that most of them are compensated and regulated by counter-motifs that function in a more systemic and totalising fashion: for example, the ethnographic representation of the social – or the interests of lobbyists – can at times be overlooked due to the pressures and demagogic tyranny of a direct democracy of surveys and hot lines.

However, the notion of the public has become even more complex through yet another mode: as an adjective, it has expanded the territory it claims and the poles it seeks to hold. If the plurality of the publics can be illustrated as the fragmentation of the receiver end of the sender-receiver model, it can also be construed as a monopoly on the different positions of the communicational diagram. In the first case the public is being spelled as a plural noun *publics*. It designates a list of potential or actual receivers, susceptible to fill, concurrently or simultaneously, the role of receiver in a communicational diagram. From that single position, and through a process of feedback and dialectic interplay of reception and production, the publics have an impact on the entire structure of communication. In the second case, in its adjective form, *public* ends up qualifying almost each and every aspect of the communicational structure.

To understand this further, let us consider the distinction introduced by Mikhail Bakhtin to Roman Jakobson's communication diagram. Rosalind Krauss has already suggested, in a statement against the often reflectionist interpretations of social art historians, that Bakhtin's modifications open a new understanding of how the social enters the realm of art. Bakhtin breaks the univocal functioning of the sender-receiver model and presents a dialogical model, wherein meaning is constructed rather than given. Jakobson's model offered the following configuration:

	content	
sender	message	receiver
	contact	
	code	

Bakhtin reformulated it as follows:

	object	
speaker	utterance	listener
	intertext	
	language	

The two most important substitutions involve the intertext for contact, and language for code, replacing the unidirectional nature of communication flow in the earlier diagram with two-way terms.[2]

Now, to test how the public-as-adjective has come to expand on the territory mapped by these models, I propose that you keep in mind the series of controversies that have taken place around the National Gallery of Canada since the purchase of Barnett Newman's *Voice of Fire*. It includes fierce battles against the exhibition of Jana Sterbak's *Flesh Dress*, the purchase of a Mark Rothko painting and, to a lesser degree, the purchase of Guido Reni's *Jupiter and Europa*.

Initially, the issue of the public re-entered artistic practices as concerns about context/object. Even within these positions, the term has expanded its claim. The critique of modernism, it has been argued, has been supported to a large extent through a return of concerns for referentiality and extra-artistic content. The dissolution of boundaries between the private and public has entailed a dramatic and quite justified inflation in the number of private topics (largely centred around gender and sexual identity)

seeking acknowledgement as part of the public realm. Dismissed is the notion that the public content of art should concern only the account of public matters (dealing with a narrow definition of the political). The expansion of what was to be considered public content was accompanied by an expanding perimeter of what constituted public space. For example, the first so-called public interventions were labelled by the fact they were presented outside of the museological institution. This is an interesting reversal since the museum, along with salons, had been one of the first contexts for the public viewing of art. Both museums and salons had been influential in the very emergence of the notion of the public, as Thomas Crow has very well demonstrated.[3] The implications of that reversal were that the presentation of art in public spaces or private non-institutional settings allowed a larger public to view it.

What the recent controversies have made very clear is that there is no longer any space for art that is not public, at least in Canada. The attacks against the National Gallery stemmed from the conviction that the institution with its national mandate was obliged to symbolically represent the taste of the Canadian public (no matter how impossible this was to achieve in reality) or at least not to offend it. We can foresee the day where every space will be public, even the private commercial galleries, as far as they are exhibiting artists who receive grants dispensed with *public funds*. For this new line of thought is now the most operative one in the discussion of art and the public, as debates around Jana Sterbak in Canada, or Robert Mapplethorpe in the United States, have made painfully clear. We then witness an adjunct consequence of the adjective 'public': it serves to qualify not so much 'public' space or 'public' content, but the awakening of the public in the guise of the taxpayers discovering themselves as the principal aesthetic sponsor of the country's cultural production. One should not be surprised to see that the most ferocious charge against art began with this change of hats. For, as a sponsor, the taxpayer does not see him or herself as the mere receiver of information; he or she challenges the position of the sender/ speaker, a position whose function is, as Jakobson pointed out, expressive or emotional. It is from that position mainly that the issue of possible censorship is raised as a threat.

There are two remaining positions in the communications diagram. Consider the role of language. Here again the problems of the National Gallery of Canada are revealing. Abstraction is not a shared language, so although the Guido Reni purchase was more expensive, it did not provoke the outrage that was triggered by the purchase of Newman's *Voice of Fire*. (I would even argue that if the Rothko did not instigate the same furious reaction, it was not because that scenario had already been played out around Newman, nor that the media do not like *déjà vu* situations, nor that the National Gallery had become more strategic in its announcement. It also differed because a geometric painting by Newman speaks less of a shared language than the more atmospheric and lyrical abstraction of a work by Rothko.) As for the intertext, it goes without saying that the public has a share in it: intertext is the locus of an ambiguous rendezvous between speaker and listener, the real ground of the dialogical construction of meaning. This is the position to which the speaker formulates his or her utterance and from which the listener receives meaning from what is being uttered. Almost inescapably, what is received does not coincide exactly with what has been formulated, whence another displacement, and the cycle repeats itself throughout the communication process.

The configuration emerging from that overwhelming expansion of the public-as-adjective threatens a complete appropriation of the communication structure, a public monopoly of the artistic situation. Yet, here is a position of resistance, encircled on all sides – which is the message. The message/utterance, as a single material statement, enjoys a peculiar status in this repositioning of 'the public'. Not only is it the position to which the public has no claim; it is the very position from which the public tends to exclude itself. Here again, the controversies, as expressed in the doxological voice of the newspapers, are quite telling. If people refuse to see *Voice of Fire* or the *Flesh Dress* as art, it is because anybody, usually a child they know, could do the same – art is what they cannot do. The message of public outcry around art, therefore, embodies the very position the public idealises as one it is impossible to occupy, turning its own exclusion from it as a primary condition of the public definition of art and of public tolerance and acceptance of what is being produced under that name. Precisely at the point where it stops, the expansion of the public-as-adjective reveals the élitist and modernist credo to which the public still wishes to hold the artist.

This is why the insistence of *Queues, Rendezvous, Riots: Questioning the Public* to anchor its question in the materiality and the possibility of the public marker – and of the figures and affects it is likely to stimulate – seemed indeed a very relevant question, and one the curators knew could not be answered there and then, at Banff in the summer of 1992. It is not merely a rhetorical question, certainly is it bound to be an open one.

Notes

1 Rosalind Krauss, 'Reading Cubism', *Picasso and Braque: A Symposium*, Museum of Modern Art, New York, 2 November 1989.

2 *ibid*, p275, for a detailed discussion of the differences.

3 Thomas Crow, *Painters and Public Life in Eighteenth-Century Paris*, Yale University Press, New Haven and London, 1985.

Sealed June 16, 1994

Half an ounce of oak wood
chippings,
volume two of Karl Marx's
Capital (mint condition,
Progress Press edition),
one brown button,
three cola bottles (circa 1990),
lots of paper clips,
thirty-seven cents in pennies,
assorted chop-sticks,
a woman's left boot,
a woman's right boot (non-
matching),
not too many men's black
plastic combs,
a child's compass,
Richard Nixon's resignation
speech,
one copy of "Bulgaria on Five
Dollars a Day,"
no men's ties,
and forty-three or forty-four
other items.

MARK LEWIS
COLLECTION

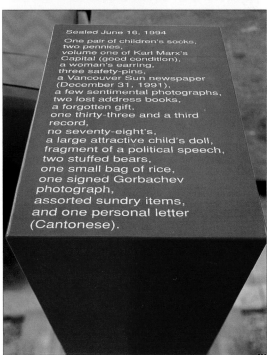

Sealed June 16, 1994
One pair of children's socks,
two pennies,
volume one of Karl Marx's
Capital (good condition),
a woman's earring,
three safety-pins,
a Vancouver Sun newspaper
(December 31, 1991),
a few sentimental photographs,
two lost address books,
a forgotten gift,
one thirty-three and a third
record,
no seventy-eight's,
a large attractive child's doll,
fragment of a political speech,
two stuffed bears,
one small bag of rice,
one signed Gorbachev
photograph,
assorted sundry items,
and one personal letter
(Cantonese).

The project features two types of works which though formally similar, operate differently:
Collection *was installed in Vancouver in November 1994 and confronts some of the expectations currently surrounding the* idea *of public art, referring to 'the monument which continues to inform the expectations and legibility of most public works'. The steel containers in* Refuse *are actual refuse collectors: the concrete bases recall the idea of a plinth (with the steel wedge acting as a 'monument').* Collection *functions as conduits for the 'preservation' of discarded and waste objects, parodying the idea of archaeology and historical recovery.*
[Thanks to Mark Wasuita for assisting with the realisation of this project – ML]

THE AUDIENCE FOR A PIECE OF SILENT MUSIC
CHRISTIAN MARCLAY
Russell Ferguson

Christian Marclay's *Amplification* was installed last summer in the Church of San Stae, Venice, as part of the Swiss participation in the 1995 Venice Biennale. On entering the church, the viewer found the nave of the church filled with six large sheets of translucent cotton scrim suspended from the ceiling. Each of these scrims bore the enormously enlarged reproduction of a snapshot of an amateur musician or group of musicians. Around the edge of the church, each of the six altars that line the nave had placed upon it, just off-centre, one of the original snapshots, simply framed. To what extent can this piece be considered a piece of public art? Although it was an official part of the Biennale, and thus drew the international art audience that fills Venice for that event, it was located away from the relatively isolated site of the national pavilions. The Church of San Stae is near the Ca d'Oro, and is easily accessible to a somewhat more general audience.

Churches in general have an ambivalent relationship to the public, especially in a tourist centre such as Venice: open to anyone who chooses to enter, they serve as a place for the public acknowledgement of private life: marriages, funerals, even confession. The appearance of personal life in a public context is a theme that would be present in *Amplification* even without this context. The content of the photographs – musicmaking – seems to call for an audience, for someone to acknowledge this transitory art. But all these musicians played in private, at most for a few friends or family members. And the circumstances of their photographs' journey to San Stae – abandoned to fleamarkets, where the artist picked them from among heaps of junk – locks them inevitably into a narrative of loss and resurrection. The photographs themselves were thrown away, flimsy testaments to the passage of those shown in them out of human memory. Their reappearance here does not restore individual identity to their subjects, but their new, monumental scale makes a claim instead to a public level of attention for these records of private performance.

Although *Amplification* was made for installation in the Church of San Stae, it was not tied strictly to that site alone. Instead it hovered somewhere between private memory and public space, much as the huge but fragile scrims hovered in the nave. As the light changed, the suspended images passed in and out of transparency, and as they did so, the church's own architecture and decoration was intermittently visible through the scrim. Since the interior included the tall pipes of the organ and many depictions of musicmaking, for which the church was well known, the links between the work and its context were close. In the end, it is perhaps a kind of hybrid, fluctuating between an autonomy unrelated to its (ambivalently) public site and at the same time entering into an intimate dialogue with it.

Christian Marclay, Amplification, *Church of San Stae, Venice, 1995, mixed media installation with six found photographs and six photographic enlargements on cotton scrim. Photo (overleaf): Pierre Antoine Grisoni, CH-Morges*

BURN OUT (THE SMASHED CAR PARK)

Henrik Plenge Jacobsen and Jes Brinch

This work was made for 'Wonderful Copenhagen's' summer festival for art in public spaces called 'Art in City 94', which is organised as a co-operation between the municipality of Copenhagen and the Danish Tourist Board. The work consisted of 18 cars, a caravan and a public bus, placed on Kongens Nytorv, which, with its classical architecture is traditionally considered Copenhagen's most beautiful square. The exhibition was held from 15th-21st June 1994, even though it was originally intended to have lasted three months. The work was placed in a car park in front of the Hotel d'Angleterre, a former car park that had been recreated for this specific event.

The work was created to give the impression that a mad crowd had gone berserk and smashed up a public car park. The cars had hence been worked over with heavy steel tubes. In the car park itself, one of the cars had been turned on its side, another was turned upside down, whilst others were left standing on all fours wheels. Every single car had some personal objects inside to signal its owner's lifestyle. A BMW had, for example, a mobile phone and the magazine *Euroman* on the back seat, with Playboy stickers on the outside of the car. This was done to make the cars look like they were owned by real, living people. The work included a caravan which had been brutally destroyed. The most important element of the show was the number 31 bus, one of the regular Copenhagen buses, placed to give the impression that it had been dragged from the nearest bus stop and turned over during the riot.

The intention was that the work should look as real as possible, to make people stop and stare aghast. The normal, well known cityscape is the archetypal symbol of ordinary, common reality, where everything happens by fixed rules. We wanted to break this 'normality' by creating this anarchistic action in the 'Wonderful Copenhagen/Art in City' context. The car park gave the impression that society had momentarily broken down. We were happy that the work had crossed over from the closed art circles to the public reality, so that it could be seen by all kinds of people. That the work was presented on Kongens Nytorv by 'Wonderful Copenhagen/Art in City' gave the work an official status, adding an extra bizarre dimension to the work – after all, who would expect the Tourist Board to smash up cars in a public car park to celebrate the city of Copenhagen's birthday?

But this is not the end of the story. Even before the official opening things began happening. We placed the bus and the cars on Kongens Nytorv the night before the official opening. First the bus was placed on its side, so that it rested on the side with the doors. This was done with great care, so that no windows in the bus were broken, not even those facing the ground. We left Kongens Nytorv on the Tuesday night at midnight, to return the next day at 10.00am. By then, every window in the bus had been broken and the interior was completely destroyed. Two cars had not only been turned upside-down but also had been moved from their original places. All this had happened during the night. A VW had been pushed about 100 metres away by children from a nursery class and their teacher in broad daylight. The opening on Wednesday caused no problems. But the same night the destruction continued. Random passers-by continued to destroy the cars during the night. And this continued the following night, which made 'Wonderful Copenhagen' employ a watchman to look after the place, after several complaints from Hotel d'Angleterre. This did not stop people from smashing the cars; all it meant was that there was somebody there to prevent them from beating each other up, and from pushing the damaged cars out onto the street which would have created traffic problems.

The fact that people continued to destroy the cars came as something of a surprise. We did not expect the work to be provocative enough to make people run amok in a public and heavily trafficked place, where there were witnesses present at all times. However, we did not see these reactions as a problem. We had created the work according to our idea of what a smashed car park looked like, and now the events and the public showed us what it looked like in reality: the work had changed from being an idea and a work of art to a reality. The fact that people used the work was in our opinion the best that could happen. Our intention was that the work should be public, for everybody, a work of art that the public could do with as they desired.

The result was a fuss in the Danish media and a lot of letters to the newspapers, asking the question: 'Is this supposed to be art?' along with many demands that the work should be removed. The papers had letters from two Danish right-wing politicians that stated that the work cast a stain on the city of Copenhagen's honour. The majority of the press were of the opinion that we were fake artists, that we did not create art, and that we only made the work to gain as much attention as possible from the media.

On Monday, June 20th, we were invited to a meeting with 'Wonderful Copenhagen'. We were informed of the situation: political pressure had been put on 'Wonderful Copenhagen' to make them remove the work. This pressure came from the Chief Mayor of Copenhagen, Jens Kramer Mikkelsen, who had opened the show himself, from those within 'Wonderful Copenhagen', from the Bank of Denmark and from representatives of business in central Copenhagen. We were asked how we would react to the removal of the work, to which we replied that we would protest, consider it censorship, and that we wanted the work to be exhibited as long as possible of the contracted exhibition period, which was three months. 'Wonderful Copenhagen' consequently informed us that they had decided on the removal of the work because 'the work had evolved into being an unintentional danger zone for passers-by because of broken glass, sharp objects and doubtful hygiene'. The same was later stated in a press release from 'Wonderful Copenhagen'.

Later that day we discovered that the bus had been removed before the meeting had been held, and that it had been a sham, since the decisions had already been made. The removal gained tremendous attention from the press, which made many journalists declare that it was in our interest to have the work removed, and again that it was only created to gain attention. We did not agree with any of these points.

The work was created to give people the possibility to see it for real, not in a newspaper or on television. We did not, at any time, wish to have the work removed, since this would have severed the possibility of communicating directly with the public on our own premises. It was in no way favourable for us to profit from a case of censorship, since this would lead to a superficial discussion of whether the work was art or not. We had not at any point calculated to gain attention by having the work removed. The work was not linguistic, but based on a direct sense experience. Hence, a discussion in the press would have been no substitute for the work itself.

In our opinion, the work hit something vital. Our opinion is that the work was removed because it invited common malicious damage and civil disobedience. The work was able to turn random passers-by into disobedient and subversive hooligans. The censorship happened because the authorities do not want it to be obvious how little it takes to make people run amok. And the authorities do not want to admit that the apparently controlled and orderly Danish society is chaotic and uncontrollable beneath the surface, and there are a lot of people that actually *feel like* running amok. This problem in society should not be repressed, but should be encouraged to emerge. That is why the work should have been left standing, and precisely why it was removed.

Our different works have one thing in common; our anarchistic way of working. We want to make the rules by which we create art ourselves. In contrast to a normal artistic project we do not aim at a continuous art production, or a strategy. On the contrary, we create a new art work every time, depending on the circumstances, not considering whether or not it continues the logic of our former works. We have no other aim than systematically attacking frozen images of reality.

Henrik Plenge Jacobsen and Jes Brinch, Burn Out (The Smashed Carpark), Copenhagen, 1994, colour photographs, 60 x 79cm. Photos (above and centre): Emmanuel Perrotin

THE FILE ROOM

Click anywhere on the image to <u>continue ...</u>

WEB-SPECIFIC WORKS
THE INTERNET AS A SPACE FOR PUBLIC ART

Miriam Rosen

Notwithstanding the allures of the Internet, this fabulous space which is not a place, which can turn time inside out and which opens an infinity of windows on an equal number of worlds is ultimately a system of telephone wires and computers that can do no more than follow orders.

It should come as no surprise, then, that 'art on the Net' is most often an electronic extension of the art we are used to seeing in more conventional, physical settings. Museums, galleries and artists' spaces have all managed to stake out their (virtual) territory, although the results are still closer to catalogues – or advertisements – than exhibitions, and even then, the quality of the images, not to mention the time that it takes to get them onto the computer screen, hardly presents an immediate threat to the book-publishing industry. As for the street, the overwhelming impression that comes from 'visiting' any number of non-institutional sites is that the outdoor art fair has also been quick to find its digitised equivalent on the Internet. The democratic dimension of the exercise can hardly be overlooked: the home-made home page can be the artist's equivalent of desktop publishing, and anyone who has access to the requisite computer tools can literally show his or her work around the world. It could even be argued that the current array of cyberschlock – everything from cat paintings to psychedelia – is actually no more disappointing than much of what passes for contemporary art among the cognoscenti. But besides the fact that this kind of vacuous expression, be it upscale or downscale, is a terrible waste of time, money and human energy, it is clear that the Internet has much more than that to offer as a creative medium.

Like a CD-ROM, an Internet site on the World Wide Web (WWW) provides images, texts and sounds in digital form, and it permits the interconnection of these different elements in such a way that the user (because it no longer makes sense to speak of a viewer, or even a spectator) is largely able to organise his or her itinerary through them. But unlike a CD-ROM with its Read Only Memory, the Internet site operates on-line, which means that every work presented on the Web is a work in progress, capable of being modified by its creator and its public alike. This open-ended interactivity is among the Web's most singular aspects, and the one that provides the real possibilities (and challenges) for contemporary artistic expression.

As sophisticated as all the new technology seems, we are probably still in the prehistory of the World Wide Web (it is difficult not to think of all the inventions, from the magic lantern to Muybridge's zoopraxiscope, that preceded the Lumière brothers'

Cinématographe and Edison's Kinetoscope just a century ago). Nonetheless, there are several projects that already show various ways that art can function in this new public space. One of the real pioneering works is Antonio Muntadas's *The File Room*, an interactive archive of cultural censorship from antiquity to the present day that went on-line in May 1994 and is now 'visited' by some 200-500 people a day. Significantly, *The File Room* was not conceived for the Internet; rather, it was developed as an installation presented in the landmark site of Chicago's former Public Library, now its Cultural Center, from 20 May – 4 September 1994.[1]

The Barcelona-born Muntadas, who has been based in New York since 1971, is a veteran of the public art sphere whose multimedia installations and other interventions call into question political and cultural institutions. According to Muntadas, *The File Room*, which he initiated at the end of 1990, was partly inspired by American debates over censorship and freedom of expression in relation to public funding for the arts. However, he explains, 'I always say that a project has public reasons and private reasons. In the case of *The File Room*, the private reason is that in 1988 I received a commission in Spain for a television programme that was supposed to be about Spanish television under Franco. I worked on it for two years, and I had a green light right until it was supposed to be broadcast, when it turned red. They paid me, but they never gave me any explanation'. This incident, Muntadas adds, became one of the first cases of censorship in his archive.

As it was physically presented at the Chicago Cultural Center, *The File Room* combined the historical form of the archive – 138 black metal filing cabinets – with its contemporary counterparts, seven computer terminals. Like the Web site, this installation (variously reincarnated at the Leipzig and Cascais Biennales, the Soros Center for Contemporary Art in Bucharest and Ars Electronica in Linz) thus allowed visitors to consult an initial bank of four hundred cases of cultural censorship that had been compiled through a year's research by student assistants in Chicago, New York and Paris. Each case, described in terms of the work involved, the incident and the final outcome, is classified by historical time period, geographical location, medium and grounds for censorship.

While the grid is quite extensive – the media in particular range from visual arts to 'digital community', by way of literature, broadcast and print journalism, performing arts and cinema – there was, and still is, a strong contemporary, American bias to the cases themselves. However, *The File Room* is anything but a closed book, so to speak, because those who consult it are asked to document new cases, with the admittedly 'utopian' intention of restoring all the images and texts that have disappeared from public view because of censorship.

'This is the step forward in relation to the other installations I've done', observes Muntadas. '*The Ball Room*, *The Press Conference* or *The Stadium* were finished the day of the opening, but *The File Room* was just starting. I see the installation itself as an artefact that acquires additional meaning as people activate it. If they consult it, contribute information to it, that means they're creating a dialogue. If *The File Room* remains passive, then it's not working'.

As Muntadas stresses, the decision to extend the physical installation of *The File Room* onto the Web was the result of this logic: 'When I have an idea for a work, the medium comes afterwards, never before'. But the electronic medium has also altered the physical work in its turn: along with the computerised archive and the forms for submitting new cases, the Internet version offers a bulletin board for exchanging comments, a bibliography and anti-censorship resource list and a group of essays which can be printed out by those who 'visit' the site. As of September 1995, 85 new cases had been received, 70 of them via the Internet. According to Muntadas, the Internet public is predictably active in the United States, 'but there have been some surprises, notably from Eastern Europe – Russia, Hungary, the Czech Republic – although it's not like in the United States. There's less dialogue: they consult the archive, but they're not active enough to send documents'.

A second Internet project with explicitly global ambitions is *The People's Choice* of Vitaly Komar and Alex Melamid. Even more than *The File Room*, this site represents an electronic adaptation of an existing work: for the past two years, Komar and Melamid, the dynamite duo of (ex-) Soviet conceptual art, have been conducting a true-false public opinion poll intended to determine popular taste in contemporary painting. Inspired by the power of the polls in American political and social life, the two gadflies, who have been living in the United States since 1978, initially intended to limit their inquiry to their new compatriots, with the idea of translating into paintings the differences in taste corresponding to different socio-cultural groups. In fact, the American poll (conducted by a *bona fide* market research firm on an equally *bona fide* sampling of 1001 individuals) showed surprisingly homogenous tastes and therefore yielded only one painting: a predominantly blue landscape with lots of water and a tiny figure of George Washington in the foreground. For exhibition purposes, this tongue-in-cheek translation of statistics, 'America's Most Wanted', was accompanied by 'America's Least Wanted' (featuring a geometric abstraction in glaring colours), plus graphic representations of the poll results, also painted by Komar and Melamid. At this point, the two artists decided to expand their project along national lines, but here too the various polls in Russia, Iceland, Kenya, China, Turkey and elsewhere were remarkably similar. 'The poll shows clearly that there's no difference in culture: most of us like blue landscapes, as close to photographs as possible. Of course we're all different, but as a mass, we're all

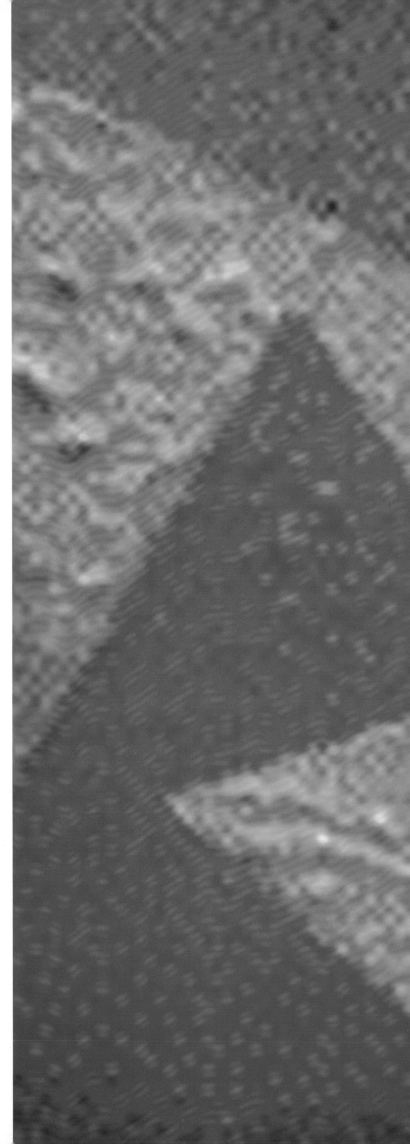

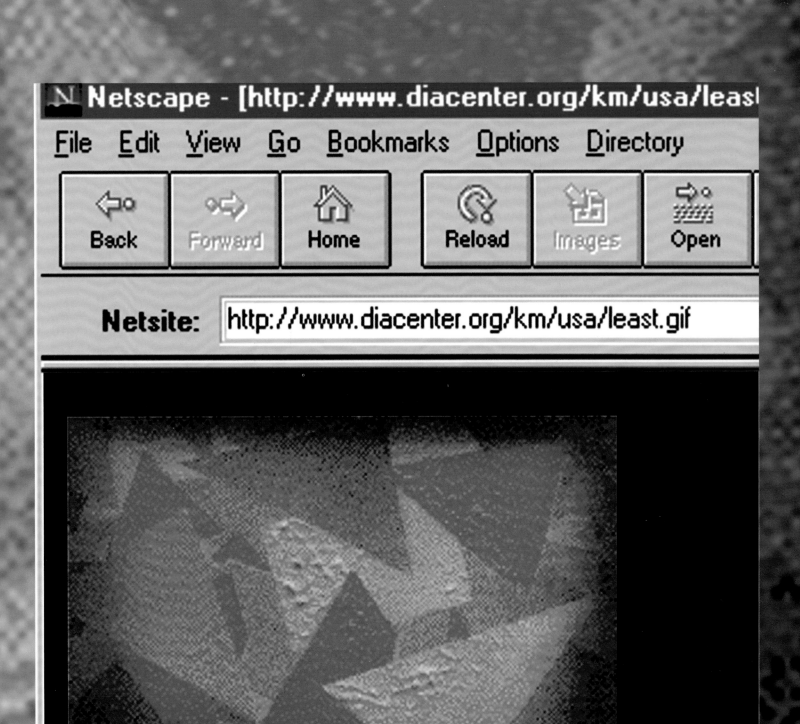

File   Edit   View   Go   Bookmarks   Options   Directory   Help

Back   Forward   Home   Reload   Images   Open   Print   Find   Stop

Netsite: http://www.diacenter.org/km/fra/most.gif

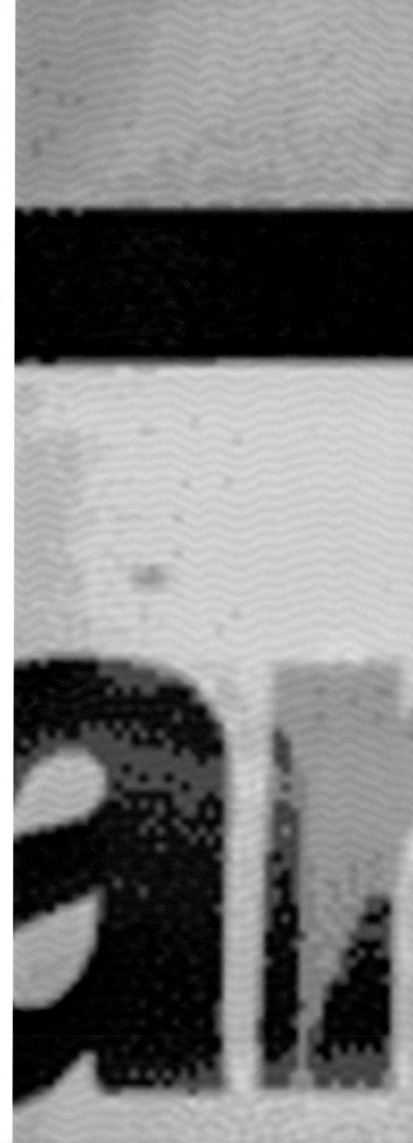

alike. That's great! There's no room for conflicts any more!' asserts Melamid, without a trace of the multiple irony that clearly informs *The People's Choice*, from the very notion of a public opinion poll and the infallibility of its interpretation to the pretended superiority of high culture. 'It's just as restricted as low culture', argues Melamid. 'In the one everybody likes blue landscapes, and in the other, Rembrandt'.

It was only last June, at the time the French poll was getting underway, that Komar and Melamid were approached by the Dia Center in New York to place *The People's Choice* on the Internet, but the two artists were quick to seize the opportunity to broaden their audience to the scale of their survey.[2] 'We see the Internet as a means of communication', stresses Melamid, 'not as a tool to produce beautiful paintings'. Indeed, like *The File Room*, the Web version of *The People's Choice* privileges the participation of the users, not only in navigating through the results of the various surveys (some 15 will have been carried out by the time the project comes to an end in 1997) but also in responding to a special poll intended to define the Internet public's 'Most Wanted Painting'. And like Muntadas, whose Internet archive on censorship already includes one case of Internet censorship (America Online's language policing policy), Komar and Melamid have clearly applied their critical vision to the functioning of the Web as well. 'It's like a good Russian soup: when you boil things too long, everything looks the same', comments Melamid, 'virtually everything is on the screen – text, pictures – it doesn't discriminate. So you don't see the contradictions any more. It loses its lustre and its flavour'. But, he adds, in one last pitch for the internationalism that also underlies *The People's Choice*, 'at least we know we're in the same soup'.

If in their respective ways Muntadas and Komar and Melamid have privileged the mass-media dimension of the Internet, two other projects bring out the possibilities for creating a kind of private public space on the Web. Here too, the end has not simply justified but preceded the means. In the case of Jenny Holzer's *Please Change Beliefs*, which inaugurated an Internet artists' space called äda 'web in May 1995, five of the artist's earlier works (*Laments*, *Truisms*, *Inflammatory Essays*, the *Living* and *Survival* series) have provided the raw material for an interactive exchange on beliefs and mentalities.[3] Holzer, another public-art veteran who got her start in the late 1970s by pasting her *Truisms* all over New York's Soho neighbourhood, moved into the electronic arena in 1982 when she was invited to display her pithy texts on the giant Spectacolor signboard over Times Square and has most recently been experimenting with virtual reality. In her view, the 'dislocation' between the simple, personal nature of her statements and their hi-tech packaging is an 'enhancement': 'It makes people look at the stuff, so I use it'.

The decision to draw on her earlier work for the äda 'web project, she explains, was dictated by a certain reality principle ('äda 'web wanted it sooner than later'), but also by the desire to explore the new medium through a familiar content. The result of

File   Edit   View   Go   Bookmarks   Options   Directory   Help

Location: **http://adaweb.com/**

welcome to ada'web
please extend your screen as far as possible
Netscape 1.1 is our prefered browser and please
turn the underline preference off

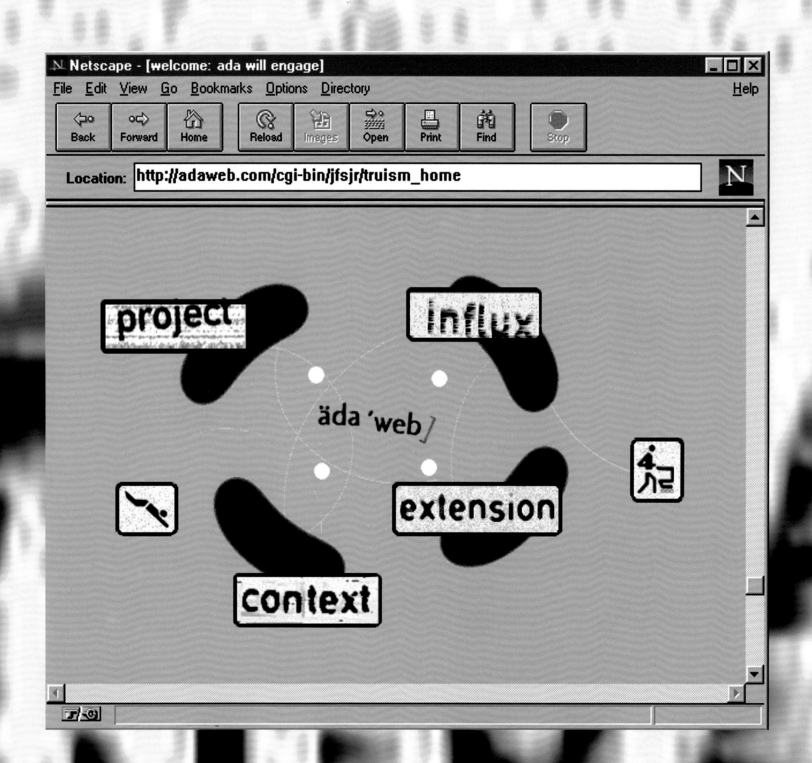

this experiment, nine months in the making, is basically the transformation of the artist's signature monologue into an open-ended dialogue with and among the site's visitors, who are first invited to acquaint themselves with a selection of truisms (the *Please* of the title), then to rework them (*Change*) and vote 'yes' or 'no' on their credibility (*Beliefs*).

Like the truisms themselves, *Please Change Beliefs* could easily be dismissed as a simplistic gimmick but turns out to be far more complex, sophisticated and serious than it first appears. The very fact of encountering Holzer's texts one by one in the physical proximity of the computer screen encourages readings – and responses – that are at once more thoughtful and more intimate. At the same time, these private reactions can be recycled into the public space of the Net for infinite rounds of metamorphosis. Holzer's classic 'Abuse of power comes as no surprise', for example, has accumulated more than 15 variants, from simple sendups like 'Abuse of computer privileges comes as no surprise' to loaded wordplay like 'Abuse of power depends on your eyes'. 'Everyone's responses are recorded, not like a poster that gets plastered over', Holzer points out, adding, 'I look all the time'.

This personalisation of the public space, which is a constant feature of Jenny Holzer's work (and a constant question in the domain of public art), is treated very differently in the last of the Web projects to be considered here, photographer Joseph Squier's *The Place*.[4] Unlike Muntadas's archive, Komar and Melamid's poll or Holzer's pool of truisms, *The Place* does not really invite the public to intervene but to experience the environment that the artist has created. While this may seem like a less ambitious undertaking, or a missed opportunity in terms of interactivity, cybercommunication and the like, it turns out in practice to provide a very welcome relief from the rhythm, the congestion and the pollution of the Information Superhighways. 'I want it to be quiet', Squier insists. 'So much of Internet is a virtual Las Vegas mentality'.

By contrast, the text-and-image works that he presents in/on *The Place* are quiet and contemplative, like very low-key CD-ROMs – an *Urban Diary*, reflections on *Life with Father*, *Anatomy* and *Outside*. Envisioned as an 'evolving repository' of Web-specific works, *The Place*, which welcomes an average of 300-500 visitors a day, has already been redesigned once since it went on-line in September 1994, and Squier intends to continue reworking it: 'The Web changes so rapidly that anything you design is soon outmoded'. But here too, his project differs from the others in that he is not collaborating with an arts institution but working within a university structure – the School of Art and Design at the University of Illinois at Urbana – where he has direct and ongoing access to the necessary equipment. 'Until now, people making electronic art have really been technicians', Squier contends. 'Now people who are primarily interested in content are able to use the tools. But you have to accept what the medium will give you. People don't understand that the Web is not watercolour'.

Ultimately, it is this fact, that the Web is not a watercolour (just as *The Place* is not an art gallery), which makes it such a propitious site for public art. If the works mentioned here emerge from a sea of electronic watercolours, it is because the artists involved, as different as their preoccupations are, have all, in the first place, had something to say, and in the second, recognised the possibilities of the Net for saying it, without getting carried away by multimedia pyrotechnics. There is no doubt that in a not-very-distant future, the text-heavy presentations of Muntadas, the elementary interface of Komar and Melamid, the halting sound and video of Holzer and the modest visual means of Squier will all seem terribly outdated. But no more so than the consumer objects that are sold in galleries and collected in museums under the label of contemporary art while the rest of the world (First, Second and Third) is receiving its news and views by satellite.

Notes

1 *The File Room* was produced by the Randolph Street Gallery in Chicago with the support of the Electronic Visualization Laboratory of the School of Art and Design at the University of Illinois at Chicago and the Chicago Department of Cultural Affairs. It has been funded by the National Endowment for the Arts, the Richard H Driehaus Foundation, the Playboy Foundation and a gift from the Goethe-Institut, Chicago. Electronic address: http://fileroom.aaup.uic.edu/FILEROOM.html

2 *The People's Choice* will remain on the Dia Center's server until the end of 1997 with major sponsoring from the Chase Manhattan Bank. Electronic address: http://www.diacenter.org

3 *Please Change Beliefs* was commissioned by äda 'web as its first special project. The site, which operates mainly through corporate funding, takes its name – and inspiration – from the musician and poet Ada Byron Lovelace, Lord Byron's daughter, who is credited with developing the first known programme for the calculating machine designed by her mathematician friend Charles Babbage. Electronic address: http://adaweb.com

4 *The Place* was produced with the support of the School of Art and Design of the University of Chicago at Urbana and the Illinois Arts Council. Electronic address: http://gertrude.art.uiuc.edu/ludgate/the/place/artist/artist.html

PAGE 86: Antonio Muntadas, The File Room, *May 1994; PAGES 88-91: Vitaly Komar and Alex Melamid,* The People's Choice, *1994;* *PAGES 92-94: Jenny Holzer,* Please Change Beliefs, *May 1995; PAGE 96: Joseph Squier,* The Place, *September 1994*

Netscape - [http://gertrude.art.uiuc.edu/ludgate/the/place/...]

File Edit View Go Bookmarks Options Directory   Help

Back Forward Home   Reload Images Open Print Find   Stop

Location: http://gertrude.art.uiuc.edu/ludgate/the/place/place2.html

manifesto   soapbox

urban diary   artist

life with father   reviews

anatomy   debt

outside   the place   ? ?